"Could there be a more timely topic [illegible] guidebook than how to grieve? Everyone still living has lost. We have lost friends. We have lost family. We have lost years of our lives. We have lost hope and faith and church and God. We have lost ourselves and we have lost our way. We have lost our bearings and lost our composure. We have nothing left . . . until we get it back again. That might take some time, and Terra McDaniel gently guides us through this period of loss during which we dare not yet even hope to regain some of what was. Is that too bleak? No. That's lament."

David McDonald, founder of Fossores Chapter House

"Terra McDaniel accompanies us into the waters of loss and lament in her book *Hopeful Lament*. She offers a helpful perspective around how we in Western society have forgotten the healing practice of lamenting. She is a faithful guide for reentering the healing practice of lament through wise and embodied ways to pray and process our sorrows. Terra doesn't shirk from the deep wounds and authentic sorrows of our day. She doesn't offer us a way around them (as if there were one), but she advocates lamenting as a way through while holding the hand of our living, loving Christ. One of the uniquely wonderful aspects of this book is Terra's inclusion of practices for families with children. We experience loss together; together we lament, and together we heal."

Lacy Finn Borgo, spiritual director and author of *Faith Like a Child*

"We all experience it—death and loss—and yet few of us know what to do with the profound grief. We have few guides. Terra McDaniel gives us that guide in her book *Hopeful Lament*. McDaniel helps us understand our grief and then journey through it with simple yet profound spiritual practices that help us find our way back to hope. She teaches us how to lament. For all who are experiencing the rawness of grief and for those who companion them, this book is for you."

MaryKate Morse, dean of Portland Seminary and author of *Lifelong Leadership*

"Lament is critical for renewal, and Terra McDaniel shows us how this courageous step connects us to the God of compassion and opens hope for recovery. This book goes about the hard but transformative work of recognizing real pain and pursuing wholeness. It is an important, heartfelt message."

Grace Ji-Sun Kim, professor of theology at Earlham School of Religion and coauthor of *Healing Our Broken Humanity*

"In no less than two seasons of life when lament and grief became a close friend, I was faced with a question: What can I do in my season of pain? Often the pain can cause us to neurotically keep busy just so we don't have to feel. That isn't the way. What so many of us need is understanding of how to constructively walk through grief in such a way that we are crawling and inching our way toward grace. This book offers a path. There is perhaps no greater a read than this."

A. J. Swoboda, associate professor of Bible, theology, and world Christianity at Bushnell University and author of *After Doubt*

"Lament and sadness go together, but they are not the same thing. Terra McDaniel poignantly shows how Christian lament is about disciplined sadness, holy prayer, formative practices, and believing in the possibility of hope without rushing to joy prematurely, all because of Christ. We will all grieve, there is a way to learn to grieve well, and this is a faithful guide and companion."

Nijay K. Gupta, professor of New Testament at Northern Seminary and author of *Tell Her Story*

"Rarely is there a friend like Terra McDaniel's book *Hopeful Lament* that can come alongside your deepest heartbreak and not try to fix it but abide with it, honor it, and give it the space it needs so that you can grow and heal in your own sacred rhythm. Reading this book gave me space to feel my grief and permission to do more than endure it. *Hopeful Lament* helped me be in relationship with my grief, letting the experience of sadness live alongside experiences of joy, delight, wonder, and hope. It is an invitation into wholeness."

Jennifer Willhoite, contemplative storyteller and artist at Cobbleworks

"Terra McDaniel has laid out a way not around but through grief—a way that is adamantly embodied and Christ centered. Like grief itself, this book will bring both tears and deep intimacy with God if you let it."

Kate Blackshear, hospital chaplain, and **Shane Blackshear**, podcaster and author of *Go and Do*

Hopeful Lament

TENDING OUR GRIEF THROUGH SPIRITUAL PRACTICES

TERRA McDANIEL

An imprint of InterVarsity Press
Downers Grove, Illinois

InterVarsity Press
P.O. Box 1400 | Downers Grove, IL 60515-1426
ivpress.com | email@ivpress.com

InterVarsity Press® is the publishing division of InterVarsity Christian Fellowship/USA®. For more information, visit intervarsity.org.

Cover design: David Fassett
Cover images: Getty Images: © Doug Armand, © stilllifephotographer, © dogayusufdokdok
Interior design: Jeanna Wiggins

ISBN 978-1-5140-0310-7 (print) | ISBN 978-1-5140-0437-1 (digital)

Printed in the United States of America ♾

Library of Congress Cataloging-in-Publication Data
A catalog record for this book is available from the Library of Congress.

30 29 28 27 26 25 24 23 22 23 | 12 11 10 9 8 7 6 5 4 3 2 1

For my grandchildren, Sutton and William. This is your story.

May you experience God's kindness

in seasons of joy and also when you encounter loss.

May you know that you are, above all else, beloved.

• • •

For my godchildren, Myles and Simone.

This is also your story. May liberation flow to and through you.

May you know and be known by Love in every step.

• • •

For all who have loved, lost, and found the courage to keep loving.

May these pages be a homecoming. May you find new ways to tend

your grief and fresh hope within and beyond it.

• • •

And for my grandson Isaiah, who we will see in heaven.

You know the fullness of which I've written

far better than I. I look forward to meeting you someday.

I'm glad you are part of our cloud of witnesses.

Contents

Introduction

When the Last Resort Is the Only Choice

Blessed are those who mourn,
For they shall be comforted.

MATTHEW 5:4 NKJV

ONE AUGUST AFTERNOON, my mother-in-law accidentally set our house on fire. The temperature was over 100 degrees Fahrenheit (38 degrees Celsius), and there was a drought. The fire hydrant near our home turned out to be broken, which made it necessary to connect with another one much farther away—that ruined any chance of saving our home. Recovering and rebuilding after that loss and countless other heartbreaks over more than a decade, I have learned to lament.

I don't believe anyone just wakes up one day with some inescapable wish to grieve. People don't study it because of its intrinsic interest. We don't want to engage it experientially because of its natural appeal. It's the kind of thing that most of us, me included, resist. Lament tends to be a last resort because it involves pain and loss and unanswerable questions.

We turn to lament when life demands it. When there is nothing else to do but sprinkle dust in our hair, rip off (and maybe tear up) garments of normalcy or celebration, and let our tears fall. If you are reading these words, you or someone you care about might be grieving something profound. My hope is that this book can be a companion as you heal and discover the life you're invited to within the grief and on the other side of what has been lost.

My encouragement is to take it all slowly. Be gentle with yourself as you enter vulnerable places. Invite a few close friends and family into what you're learning and experiencing. You might also find it helpful, even necessary, to include a trustworthy therapist or spiritual director into the process with you. Most of all, I pray you'll feel the freedom to invite the presence of the One who draws near to the brokenhearted into your experience.

Lament Is Essential

Lament tells the truth about what is. It refuses to ignore pain and injustice. It won't turn its face away from the realities of losing something or someone precious. It is an expression of love. Lament allows sorrow to be expressed, both to honor beloveds we've lost and to honor the gap left in our communities and our souls by their absence.

In the apparently ever-expanding Marvel universe, a quirky series called *WandaVision* was released in early 2021, which at first glance appears to be nothing more than a nostalgic dance through the history of sitcoms starring two superheroes. It turned out to be a thoughtful and timely means of addressing grief.

When Vision, attempting to comfort Wanda as she spoke of feeling overwhelmed by her brother's death, asked, "What is grief, if not love persevering?" the moment went viral. Many called it the defining moment of the series.[1] It's no mystery why those words resonated profoundly: Wanda's experience echoed what was happening in the world. Alisha Grauso wrote, "She has not been able to properly grieve for her compounding losses, instead forced to carry on in her duty to others, forced to carry on in her role . . . not given the chance to slow down and fully process all that she has needed to" mourn.[2]

Like Wanda, we have been grieving. You and those you love have lived through your own losses, large and small. Some of those must be healed over time. In the past several years, people I care for have experienced cancer and marriage challenges. Some have lived through the sudden death of children and marriage partners due to illness, accidents, and gun violence. Others have struggled with depression and addiction. My heart has been heavy for loved ones carrying extraordinary weights of loss and grief.

Some of you reading this have experienced the death of a loved one and are learning how to survive with the ache of their absence. Some of you are living on the other side of a heartbreaking divorce. Or you're enduring the more hidden grief of infertility or miscarriage, or a painful season of parenting when the energy and means to love your child well has been hard to find. Some of you love someone who is struggling with addiction or mental illness. You have been betrayed in your work or hurt by a church community. Some of you are being invited to bring past abuse into healing light. Others are waking up to what is yours to do to address systemic racism or human trafficking or unhoused neighbors or the ways people are harming the earth; or you're healing from the personal experience of one of those horrors. Some are living with the kind of heartache that is difficult even to whisper out loud.

I have no doubt that for some of you reading these words, if the last two paragraphs were a checklist, you would have marked it multiple times. You're living with pain and loss that touches many areas of your world, making the hard but good work of lament all the more essential but also more difficult and complex. Some of you are accompanying others through grief as a pastor, counselor, spiritual director, or other type of helper, even as you carry your own grief. And I hope you know that if what you're grieving isn't reflected here, that doesn't make it any less real and meaningful.

Lamenting What We've Lived Through Together

Beyond the undeniable weight of personal tragedies is what we've lived through together. The past years have been exhausting with crisis piling upon crisis. Our world has been decimated by a global pandemic for the first time in a century. News of a novel coronavirus began to emerge in December 2019, and only a month later the virus was declared a global health emergency.[3] Weeks after I'd jotted down that one of my hopes for the year was to travel more, people were advised to shelter in place around the world.

We started social distancing and relearning how to wash our hands. But that wasn't enough to slow the spread of the disease. By March, the World Health Organization designated the outbreak a global pandemic.[4] Children started homeschooling and adults began working from home. And as we sheltered in place and prayed that we and those we love wouldn't get sick, some of them did. Many lost friends or family, often without a chance to say goodbye. Funerals became small affairs, sometimes without being able to gather in person.[5]

A little over a year after the first whispers of a new illness originating in Wuhan, China, nearly 125 million people had gotten sick and 2,746,397 had died.[6] Life expectancy in the United States had declined by a full year due to Covid-19, the largest drop since World War II.[7] The losses were more extreme for people of color, with Black Americans' life expectancy dropping by over two and half years and Hispanic Americans' dropping by nearly two years. By March 2021, over 500,000 Americans had died from Covid-19, more than the number who died in World War I or II or in the Korean or Vietnam wars.[8]

And the tragically steady diet of disasters has been exacerbated by hate, violence, racism, fear, and division. Families and friendships have been disrupted by very different understandings of events, fueled by social media echo chambers and conspiracy theories. It all brings to mind Jesus' chilling proclamation that "one's foes will be members of one's own household" (Matthew 10:36); he was echoing a passage in Micah 7 that describes widespread bribery, perversions of justice, and corruption.

Particularly for those in the United States, the #MeToo and #ChurchToo movements have served as an unmasking. And between March and June of 2020, for the first time in its history, more than half of the calls to the National Sexual Abuse Hotline were placed by minors as children were trapped at home with their abusers due to stay-at-home orders.[9]

We've also lived through what has been referred to as a racial reckoning in the United States and abroad.[10] The brokenness and evil of racism that has harmed my marginalized brothers and sisters in overt and subtle ways is not new. But the Unite the Right Rally in 2017, in which white supremacists marched in Charlottesville, Virginia, served as one flashpoint among several igniting an era of heightened awareness of racialized and police violence.[11]

In spring 2020, after an officer knelt on George Floyd's neck for over eight minutes, his very public death along with that of several other unarmed men and women of color, particularly at the hands of police, began to capture attention and outrage in a new way. Protests erupted in Minneapolis and then around the United States and globally. Reports indicate that at least fifteen, and up to twenty-six, million people in the United States participated in demonstrations.[12]

And hate crimes against Asian Americans rose by nearly 150 percent during the pandemic.[13] This was related in part to anti-Asian rhetoric associated with Covid-19. On March 16, 2021, a young white man killed eight people (six of whom were of Asian descent) at three different Atlanta massage parlors.[14]

Meanwhile, Syria has been at war for a decade, resulting in more than half of the country being displaced, widespread destruction, and countless lives lost.[15] Rohingya Muslims were targeted for slaughter in Myanmar.[16] The Israeli-Palestinian conflict was reignited with deadly results, including for children.[17] The psalmist's cry of "How long, O Lord" is as achingly timely as ever (Psalm 13:1-2).

All that pain and death and division and destruction touching so many areas of life. Even reading about these events may have left you with a weight on your chest or a lump in your throat. Of course, I've left out countless details and important facts. And all this doesn't include your own experience of loss, but it does surface the larger context your suffering has occurred within and may shed light on why your grief might have felt particularly difficult and persistent. Which makes this a good moment, by the way, to take a deep breath, let your shoulders drop, and say a quiet prayer for yourself and all who have lived through these personal and corporate griefs.

We need to know how to lament. We need to know it is possible to engage safely, that grief can be practiced in a way that does not overpower but rather frees us. If we refuse to lament, we will not be able to move on without carrying brokenness, or trauma, that will replay unprocessed pain in and around us. Lament is about giving grief—and the love hidden within it—a way to be expressed so that it doesn't end up doing violence to us or those around us. In that way, lament is a life-affirming gift.

How We Forgot Lament

But many of us in the West have forgotten how to lament. It didn't happen overnight. The word, and so it seems its practice, slipped away slowly.[18] *Lament* and similar words like *mourn*, *grieve*, and *sorrow* started appearing in English literature less and less frequently starting in 1800. Around the year 2005, they all dropped off even further to become virtually nonexistent on our pages, leaving a gap in the way grief and loss are (not) processed. I think this reveals something important about our cultural willingness, and even our capacity, to face and process pain.

There has been a slight resurgence of lament and related terms in recent years in American publications. But the gap remains.

Part of the absence of lament might have to do with the fact that we tend to live longer and (thank God) must bury fewer of our children than was true before the nineteenth century; but fewer is not none. If you are mourning the loss of a child, my prayer is that you'll feel held in the ache of your grief. Our discomfort with sorrow is likely also connected to an Enlightenment sense of independence and greater disconnection from communities that both celebrate and mourn together. Charles Taylor points out that in the premodern world "the common weal [good] was [understood to be] bound up in collective rites, devotions, allegiances."[19] This is much less true in our hyper-individualized society. Loneliness was being called an epidemic even before years of extraordinary isolation and disconnection due to the pandemic.[20] Since processing the pain associated with complex losses can begin as an individual endeavor but doesn't often remain so, our separation has made it harder for us to grieve well.

There is no doubt that our widespread amnesia with respect to lament also has to do with the obsession with forward thinking and positivity that characterized much of the twentieth century in the West. The belief that humanity was destined to keep getting better was shaken but not broken by things like the Spanish flu, the Great Depression, and two world wars. Along with an overreliance on optimism, a resistance to and even denial of negative emotions grew within parts of the church as well as the larger culture. As Henri Nouwen said, "Who wants to be reminded of their weaknesses and limitations, doubts and uncertainties? Who wants to confess that God cannot be understood, that human experience is not explainable?"[21]

But loss and suffering and uncertainty are part of life. To deny the hard ultimately also diminishes the beautiful. In the Christian story, death comes before resurrection. As John O'Donohue wrote, "Light cannot see inside things. That is what the dark is for: minding the interior, nurturing the draw of growth through the places where death in its own way turns into life."[22]

Lament refuses to bury pain or, just as dangerous, to give in to despair. It is an ancient practice lost in many modern contexts, at least among grownups who feel awkward wailing in public. And it's essential to embrace in a season of abundant loss and pain. Grief is sometimes framed as negativity or immature faith, but it is vital we be present to sorrow before healing can be sustainable.

Engaging Lament

It is high time to reclaim the gift many of us have lost. We must rediscover what has been forgotten. Some, particularly among the marginalized and oppressed, never lost the practice of lamenting because the realities of their lives didn't allow it. Part of the good work ahead will be to continue learning from the hard-won wisdom of those who have faced grief head on. And for all of us, it is to remember that God welcomes the full range of our experience. It's human to celebrate. And it's just as human to grieve when there's suffering or injustice. Lament is more than mentally acknowledging the reality of loss or pain.

It's holding our grief and letting ourselves fully experience it instead of numbing or ignoring it, hoping it will go away. It's about tuning into the emotional and embodied experience of heartache and bringing all of that into the loving presence of the Holy.

Each chapter that follows includes stories of how engaging lament can help you and your loved ones heal, and offers practices to try. My hope is that you will add your own wisdom and experience and creativity to practicing lament as you go. I encourage you to experiment, coming up with ways that work for you. And please invite trusted friends and community into all of it. There is power and healing in sharing our pain with others and with the Spirit.

Lament isn't a magic wand or a one-time fix. It is a *practice* we're invited to: embodied rituals to return to as often as we need, layered in with other habits of grounding and prayer that help us connect with God and our own souls. Lament can address personal pain and losses. And it is something we can practice together when facing communal losses.

As you proceed, remember that lament is heavy lifting. It is restful in one very real sense because it means we're not denying or distancing from what's really happening. But at the same time, it can be hard and even scary work at times. With its complexity and unknowns, it might feel like grief will overwhelm you because it's so big at times.

That means engaging lament will sometimes require a surprising measure of energy. There might be moments when you are tempted to bury this book and forget it. You might even be tempted to throw it across the room. It will mean cultivating resilience to engage complicated and painful emotions. As you stay with me in reclaiming (or going deeper into) the difficult yet indispensable act of practicing lament, trust it will be worth it.

Jan Richardson, a contemplative Christian well acquainted with grief, wrote that loss might require some undoing. She said, "Some things you have protected may want to be laid bare . . . though it may be hard to see it now, . . . this is where you will receive your life again."[23] I encourage you to dip your toes in and take small sips of these things. Be gentle with yourself. Allow lament to become part of a rhythm of practices that help you stay present to what's true, while remaining connected to grace and hope. Whatever your history, wherever you come from, you are welcome to this good and holy and necessary work.

And know this—lament is surprisingly hopeful. As strange as that may sound now, I promise it's true. It's an act of trust both that we can face pain and survive, and that God cares about our anger, confusion, doubt, grief, and fear. And when we're not stuck suppressing or spiraling in grief, we're freed up to act for goodness and freedom and justice.

1

Ashes for Beauty

Before you know kindness as the deepest thing inside,
You must know sorrow as the other deepest thing.
You must wake up with sorrow.
You must speak to it till your voice
Catches the thread of all sorrows
And you see the size of the cloth.

NAOMI SHIHAB NYE

AS THE FLAMES OF OUR HOUSEFIRE were making their way through my daughter's carefully preserved keepsakes and the shelves of our beloved books, our ordinarily cranky neighbor stood outside sobbing for us. My dazed father-in-law wandered around the yard looking for his socks. And I was barefoot in 100-degree heat, holding my phone.

In the midst of the chaos, I tweeted a message from the book of Job: "The Lord gives, and the Lord takes away. Blessed be the name of the Lord" (Job 1:21 CSB).

I must have been in shock. I remember cracking a joke with our youth pastor as orange flames roared through the roof and blackened the limestone walls of our home. He wore the blank expression of a deer in headlights, while I was recalling a funny moment from several years prior. On that earlier night, the fire department had been erroneously summoned when commuters noticed an unexpectedly lively bonfire, meant for spiritual contemplation and roasting s'mores, in our backyard. I imagine I sounded crazed to chuckle while my house was being consumed behind me. Or maybe I seemed flippant, like I couldn't care less about what was happening.

When I think about that post today, I'm not sorry I shared it. But just as that proclamation was only the beginning of Job's journey through pain and loss and sometimes misguided comforters, so it was for my family and me. I think where people of faith often get it wrong is to stop with praise or trust like Job's. Or, just as harmful, to fast-forward to Job's encounter with God that leads to his confession of God's sovereignty and power, which is quickly followed with his restoration. As if the lives of his newborn children could replace his sons and daughters who died. As if all that came in between—the aching and the questions and confusion—are incidental. They aren't. They are essential parts of a mysterious and perplexing story with a troubling end. And I love that the Bible doesn't turn its face away from any of it. We do so at our peril.

An Ancient Source of Help . . . and Hard Questions

Job is a book of poetry that describes the life of a righteous man and his experience of suffering and loss. What those of us reading his story know—that Job's friends did not—is that Job was innocent. Was he, were *they*, being tormented to settle a divine argument about why Job worshiped God? Satan argued

Job was faithful because of God's provision of wealth, vitality, and family. But God maintained Job was blameless and gave Satan freedom to take everything he had—and he did exactly that. Job's oxen, donkeys, sheep, camels, and his children all died violently in a single horrific day. Messengers arrived, one after the other, to tell Job about attacking Sabeans, wildfires, Chaldeans, and windstorms.

And Job refused to blame God. He got up, tore his clothes, shaved his head, and called out, "Naked I came from my mother's womb, and naked shall I return there; the Lord gave, and the Lord has taken away; blessed be the name of the Lord" (Job 1:21). That response to suffering and loss leaves me in awe every time. I copied some of those words when my house was on fire, but I can't say that I grasp what they really mean, then or now. There is a steel and grace in them that is beyond me.

Job's and his unnamed wife's misery wasn't over yet. God again pointed out Job to the Accuser. He asked him to notice how Job still honored God and turned away from evil. Satan snorted in derision, "Take his health and you'll see how quickly he turns against you." Again, God allowed it. Job's wife told him to give up. She figured death was better than the kind of life in which the Divine seemed to want him to suffer.

Job's friends heard the news and left their homes to comfort him. From a distance, he was so disfigured they didn't recognize him. They cried for him. And then they did precisely what was needed—they met him where he was in his grief.

In the film *What Dreams May Come*, Robin Williams and Annabella Sciorra play bereaved parents trying to figure out how to live again after losing their two beloved children in a car crash. It's a story of the afterlife filled with rich images drawn from various faith traditions and literature, including Dante's visions of heaven and hell. When the mother, Annie, isn't able to cope, she commits suicide and is condemned to hell. Her husband, Chris, refuses to abandon her there and risks his sanity to try and find her.

When he does, he's struck with the revelation that it wasn't her grief but rather his refusal to allow either of them to fully mourn their children that separated them. Sitting with her in what looks like the ruins of their home on earth, he recognizes he was part of the problem; "Not because I remind you [of them]. But because I couldn't join you."[1] In the film, his belated willingness to meet her in the fullness of her grief and engage his own unlocks a healing connection that ultimately frees them both.

Like Chris, Job's friends didn't simply observe from a polite distance. They joined him in his grief. They tore their robes as Job had rent his. They covered themselves with dust as he was covered in ashes. They sat with him in silence. After a week, Job was ready to say something.

And what he said is breathtaking. He cursed the day of his birth—because never having lived seemed better than surviving within his loss and pain. Or if he must have been born at all, why couldn't he have died at birth since he would be with those who were now at rest? He wailed, "Why is light given to one who cannot see the way, whom God has fenced in? For my sighing comes like my bread, and my groanings are poured out like water. Truly the thing that I fear comes upon me, and what

I dread befalls me" (Job 3:23-25). His cries of agony will be familiar to all who have known grief. His words and his actions are part of the excruciating truth-telling that grief requires: it's called lament.

Moving Through Grief

It's never a good sign when people start comparing your life to a biblical figure known for pervasive suffering. But that's what started happening to my family a few years before our house fire. Things were falling apart, and our once tight-knit family connections were significantly strained.

We had just reached a new, more-settled normal and were trying to embrace hope for the future. My daughter and I had just gotten matching tattoos of the word *hope* alongside a swallow in flight, inspired by Psalm 62:5-6. And then, our house burned to the ground. We had much to lament.

Ancient practices like Job's, lost or forgotten in many modern cultures, also appear in the Gospel story of Jairus's daughter. That's the story of a local synagogue leader who seeks Jesus' help for his ailing daughter. Matthew, Mark, and Luke all tell the story of Jesus agreeing to help and following Jairus toward his home before being interrupted by another healing, that of a woman who'd been hemorrhaging for twelve long years. After pausing to affirm her faith, Jesus continued on his way.

But it was too late. When they arrived at the leader's home, the girl had already died. Their friends and neighbors had gathered to grieve, crying loudly and playing music to mark her loss. When Jesus told the mourners she wasn't dead, their tears vanished and they started laughing. In the past, I assumed their performance of grief was by definition insincere and took their apparently mocking laughter as evidence of that fact. Similar practices of enacting grief, like wearing rough clothing, tearing garments, and pouring on ashes, also seemed inauthentic and overly dramatized to me.

But I've come to believe that practices like these and the inner healing work they're connected with are essential. Lament is more than mentally acknowledging the reality of loss or pain. It's holding our grief and letting ourselves fully experience it instead of numbing or ignoring it, hoping it will go away. Spoiler—it won't.

Lament is carrying our questions and complaints before the Spirit of God. It is expressing pain in an embodied way where it doesn't turn into violence directed at ourselves or anyone else. And there's no question it's something many of us have to learn how to do. James K. A. Smith says, "Mourning takes practice."[2] It doesn't come naturally to most of us.

But the alternative is to bury our grief or anguish so that it becomes toxic to ourselves or those around us. This can be true for individuals and families, and even entire nations. Pain can make us so hypervigilant about avoiding more of it that we miss out on life around us. Grief can make it harder to learn from our mistakes.[3] Unresolved pain and anxiety can cause us to exaggerate the risk of bad outcomes.[4] Trauma is intense grief related to an overwhelming event or series of experiences. It changes us physically: recalibrating our brains, increasing stress hormones, altering systems that help us distinguish relevant and irrelevant input, and "compromises the brain area that communicates the physical, embodied feeling of being alive."[5] When you remember trauma, your body experiences it as if it's happening again.[6]

Therapist Resmaa Menakem distinguishes between what he calls "clean pain" and "dirty pain." Dirty pain avoids, blames, and denies. It is an overflow of unhealed wounds that makes people prone to lash out or run away. It always creates more suffering. Clean pain still hurts, of course, but it is pain that can mend and create growth. When "the body metabolizes clean pain, the self becomes freer and more capable," with access to insight and energy no longer needed to focus on grief.[7] Lament is clean pain. It is a way of taking ourselves as whole people—with bodies, souls, and spirits—seriously.

Permission to Grieve

I'm sorry to say that I used to disparage stories of people escaping fires without taking as much as a photo album with them. *If it were me, I'd grab at least a few important papers or family photos,* I'd think to myself, not realizing how cold and unkind or downright wrong I was. When I heard my mother-in-law yelling, clearly frightened, I stepped out of my bedroom and saw a wall of orange flame outside the kitchen window. I raised my eyes farther and saw sparks beginning to shower into our study that held a collection of books my husband and I had been carefully curating since we'd gotten married two decades before.

I'd just thrown on clothes after showering, so I was stepping outside with wet hair and bare feet. I had time to make sure my family was outside and to grab my purse and our twenty-five-pound French bulldog. My hands were shaking so badly I struggled to dial 911. Thankfully, a police officer, and surreally a friend of my daughter's, were both arriving at our doorstep as my in-laws and I opened the door to exit. Because the fire was visible from a nearby roadway, they and others, including the bewildered youth pastor, had come to make sure we were getting to safety.

Firefighters, who were incredibly hardworking and kind, were on their way. Kyle was stuck in traffic on his way home from work, and Torey was a few hours away working as a camp counselor. I might have been able to run in briefly for more than my wallet, but as we began to walk away from the flames there was a terrifying moment when we couldn't find my father-in-law. We discovered him trying to put out the fire with a garden hose even though the blaze was clearly well beyond that possibility. We now realize it is likely that he was in the early stages of dementia and had gotten confused in all the commotion.

Between the drought and the malfunctioning hydrant, the fire was catastrophic. We lost almost everything. My daughter's baby clothes and toys we'd saved for her future children were all gone. The roof over her bedroom had been entirely consumed, revealing a bright sky. The contrast between the cheerful blue sky dotted with puffy white clouds above and the charred remains below was jarring.

A quilt created by a beloved small group when we'd moved away from Houston was blackened and tattered. The Bible I'd used for prayer and study for over a decade, which was filled with notes and dates I'd prayed passages for whom and why, was lost. I couldn't find my wedding ring. Still, we were exceedingly thankful that no lives had been lost, including that of our beloved dog, who would have been left home alone while we went out to dinner if the fire had started even a few minutes later than it did.

And *people showed up* to care for our family in incredible ways. They came the next morning to help us salvage what could be saved. Friends traipsed through the rubble to search for mementos—one found my wedding ring in our entry hall under a pile of insulation where fire hoses had propelled it fifty feet from next to the kitchen sink where I'd left it. Another family gathered up our dishes and took them to our neighbors' yard to carefully rinse them off with their garden hose. Others wiped off countless photographs, taken in those days before smartphones made printed photos relics, and laid them to dry. Others made us meals.

One kindhearted couple even took us in, and we lived with them until we figured out short-term housing. I'll never forget the mom who took my daughter shopping before her sophomore year of college began, for clothes to replace those she'd lost. We were deeply loved and cared for in that season and we will be forever grateful.

Everything Happens for a Reason?

People tried to encourage us that "God would work it all for good." About the fire, people said, "It's just stuff." They told us, "Aren't you so glad you have faith, you *know* everything's going to be okay? You *know* it happened for a reason." But we didn't know everything was going to be okay. We didn't know that it had happened for a reason. We didn't know what to think. A few years later, I came across a greeting card that read, “Please let me be the first to punch the next person who tells you everything happens for a reason. (I’m sorry you’re going through this.)”[8] I promptly bought the card and have held on to it ever since.

I know they meant well. But words like those didn’t do us any good. They were salt in our wounds. We needed to learn to lament, to stay with our pain and our exhaustion and not pretend everything was okay. But we didn’t have the language or the tools or the permission. Many people of faith were encouraging us to fast-forward to happiness and joy. They wanted us to trust in God’s sovereignty without asking the hard questions that the circumstances of our lives required. Responses like that are all too common when people encounter hardship and suffering.

God’s greatness is very good news, but it is not the answer to human suffering. God’s power and wisdom don’t erase the grief of a parent who has lost a child. It doesn’t assuage hunger or sickness. It doesn’t diminish the stark realities of war or division. Believing God is good and able isn’t a magic wand to wave away pain in the here and now. The hope of future consolation, vital as it is, doesn’t negate the realities of grief in the present.

But like Job’s friends, many modern would-be comforters find it hard to stay with others who are experiencing intensely painful emotions after the initial crisis. Faith communities who embrace what Barbara Brown Taylor calls “full solar spirituality” tend to stress certainty, positivity, and an expectation of an unwavering sense of God’s presence. The trouble starts when things go wrong in career, marriage, or parenthood. When someone begins trying to make sense of where God is and why bad things happened (or good things didn't), there is often room for questions at first. But Taylor says those who continue asking them will "be reminded that God will not let you be tested beyond your strength [and that] all that is required of you is to have faith."[9] And those whose suffering or uncertainty continue are sometimes told their problems are evidence of weak faith.

N. T. Wright calls perspectives like these a version of ancient pagan thinking. It goes something like this: God must have specifically orchestrated any bad thing that happens because he's responsible for everything. And if he does, it has to be because he's mad about something. When suffering is pervasive, as it was at the advent of the pandemic, language around God's sovereignty tends to equate it with judgment.

As it was for us, these kinds of messages are often delivered with good intentions. But they fall woefully short. I know countless people who have been accused of somehow contributing to their miscarriage, infertility, or family member's death. And many who were told to stop grieving and just believe God needed another [insert something their loved one was known for] in heaven. Messages like that are anything but harmless and often do real and lasting damage.

Wright contends Jesus "was unveiling a different meaning of divine sovereignty. *This is what it looks like*, he was saying as he healed a leper, or as he announced forgiveness on his own authority to a penitent woman."[10] He was revealing God's sovereignty when he befriended all the wrong people, went to

Jerusalem knowing he would be arrested, and when he hung on the cross. He was embodying God's sovereignty when he sweat blood in the garden and when he showed up alive after his resurrection.

Before our time of upheaval, I had been hearing a lot about God as exacting Judge, disappointed Parent, and all-powerful One. Those perspectives of God felt hollow and incomplete in the face of suffering. But recognizing that my view of how God works needed to shift and grow didn't solve my grief or confusion even though it was necessary and important. In my family's season of disorientation and loss, I needed to know God as a mother hen who wanted to protect us, as Jesus describes himself in Luke 13:34; I needed to know he would weep with me, saving each tear as if it were a treasure as Psalm 56 describes, more than I needed a towering whirlwind-God bragging about how strong he was. I don't believe God swaggers around boasting about how tough and in control he is, but there are too many pastors and teachers who paint him that way. I needed to know God as the One who would "cry out like a woman in labor" on behalf of the suffering and oppressed (Isaiah 42:14).

Antidotes for Despair

It is time to recover lament as the hard but good gift it is. Lament is a crucial part of the antidote for despair and bitterness. Unprocessed grief hurts those who carry it and others around them, too.

And there have been so many unprecedented corporate traumas and losses in recent years that many of us have gotten tired of the word *unprecedented.* The sources of grief have included highly personal and also communal loss. It will not do to try and shake these things off as if they didn't happen. If we try moving on without addressing the layers of sadness and loss, they will get carried forward in destructive ways. Eugene Peterson said anyone who "fails to acknowledge and deal with suffering becomes, at last, either a cynic or a melancholic or a suicide."[11]

We often struggle to face pain. There is a partial exception for those who have lost close family members, but even then there is not often space for genuine lament that unfolds over time, nor a recognition that since grief is experienced in waves, lament must often be revisited instead of being a one-time event. And accessible wisdom on how to do that can be hard to come by. Many of us have felt stuck around how to process our own sadness on top of the suffering around us. If we are going to survive and move forward in healthier, freer ways, we must lament.

And refusing to lament bypasses holy chances to honor those whose lives were lost or changed forever by pain and loss, including yours. We owe it to them, to ourselves, and to coming generations to learn or relearn these lessons.

It will be vital to take all this in stages, with time for tuning in to what brings life and joy in the midst. Consider spending some time with the full text of Naomi Shihab Nye's poem "Kindness," which began this chapter. You can find it online or in her collection of poetry *Words Under the Words.* As you prepare to enter the difficult but necessary gift of holy mourning more fully, I hope you'll take some time to engage the prayer practice that follows. Breath prayers can help you engage the embodied wisdom of holding grief and goodness in tension.

Breath Prayer Practice

EACH CHAPTER WILL CLOSE with some practices to try on your own as well as with others, including the children in your life. These will help you continue to engage the practice of lament so that it can become a healing habit over time. Some of them may feel silly or awkward at first. I encourage you to try them anyway, noticing what works, what doesn't, and what surprises you. My hope is that you'll make these rhythms your own. It's also important to name that some of these practices may stir up strong emotions or anxiety. Know that if something doesn't feel good or if you find yourself getting overwhelmed, stop the activity and return to a gentle breath. A short walk to discharge anxious energy might also be helpful. In all these things, proceed with kindness and care with yourself and those around you.

One of my favorite practices to engage in, and to share with those I host in spiritual direction, is *breath prayer*. It is a wonderful way to "pray without ceasing" in practice (1 Thessalonians 5:17). The idea is to choose a word or phrase to silently repeat as you breathe in and out. Conscious breathing is a wonderful way to calm and ground the body. Breath prayers add a simple yet powerful layer of articulating a prayer, bringing intentionality to the natural breath with all its centrality to life.

Breath prayers are also extremely versatile. For a set-apart time of meditation, find a comfortable seat and engage a single breath prayer repeatedly, allowing your mind to drop into your heart and listening for the still small voice of the Spirit as well as your own soul. For a moving meditation, especially helpful in times of processing anxiety or grief, you can engage a breath prayer while walking outside. Breath prayers are also great on the fly during repetitious tasks that don't require much mental engagement, such as folding laundry, running errands, or paying bills. They're also a wonderful way to focus and invite the presence of the Holy before you log onto a Zoom meeting, begin a project, or respond to someone who has hurt or frustrated you.

To practice breath prayer, choose a word or phrase that expresses what you need or what you know. It could be a verse (breathe in "Be still"—breathe out "and know that I am God"); inspired by a line of a poem (breathe in "awakening to kindness"—breathe out "speaking to sorrow"); a name of God (breathe in "Yah"—breathe out "weh"); and so forth. I encourage you to try the following breath prayer.

BREATHE IN: *Here I am.*

BREATHE OUT: *Healer, meet me here.*

"Here I am" is a way that many biblical figures responded to the voice of God or to a family member (e.g., Genesis 22:11;

31:11; 46:2; Exodus 3:4; 1 Samuel 3:4-16). And it is a wonderful way to reconnect with the physical space you're in as well as your embodied presence in the moment. Remembering that the Divine is a healer, among other loving things, is always a good thing, and all the more so when treading into vulnerable territory like lament. When you are in moments of grief or pain, you might try letting your exhale be a little longer than your inhale. If you are feeling anxiety, you might allow your inhale to be a little longer. Whatever the rhythm of breathing, try to remain present with what you are really feeling rather than what you might wish you were feeling. Invite the Spirit into that place with you and notice what, if anything, shifts.

You might find it helpful to write this or another breath prayer on a note for your bathroom mirror or save it on your phone to remind you to tune into prayer, hope, and presence. I encourage you to experiment with using breath prayers in different places and postures with or without movement. I hope you'll find them a valuable tool for processing heavy emotions and all kinds of moments.

Breath Prayer Practice for Children and Families

Children often find breath prayers helpful, too. You can invite children to engage a breath prayer of their own. You could provide bubbles and invite them to blow out their prayers. Children (and adults) often find this playful way of praying meaningful. Kids may also enjoy sculpting their prayers with modeling clay or building them with blocks or Legos. My friend Lacy Finn Borgo often invites children in the transitional living facility where she offers holy listening to breathe in "God is with me" and breathe out "I am safe."

You could also try this breath prayer with the children in your life.

BREATHE IN: *God is with me.*

BREATHE OUT: *I am loved.*

2

How Grieving Got Lost

And I said to him
Are there answers to all of this?
And he said
The answer is in a story
and the story is being told.
And I said
But there is so much pain
And she answered, plainly,
Pain will happen.

PADRÁIG Ó TUAMA

When I was in fifth grade, my grandparents were visiting my dad and stepmom. Late one night, my grandfather had a massive heart attack. My dad gave his own father CPR, but it was too late. My kindhearted papaw was gone. He was an army cook during World War II. He would make me pancakes and sausage (or anything else I wanted) when I visited their home in the Texas Piney Woods. He was faithful and quiet. He was artistic; I didn't learn until well after his death that he'd created the intricate wood carving of a bird dog that hung in their den next to my grandmother's recliner.

Anytime I was staying with them, he took me to Sunday school at the Methodist church across town with its pretty stained-glass doors. He mystified me by his love of fishing for bass or catfish in the middle of the night. But that didn't stop me from enjoying the fish he'd bring home, which my mamaw would fry in cornmeal and serve with homemade hush puppies. And he was simply and suddenly absent.

I was unsettled by my grandmother's grief. When she would break into sobs out of nowhere, I did whatever I could to stop her tears. I had the idea that if I could distract her or make her laugh that was the same as comforting her. But that's not how grief works. What I didn't understand as an eleven-year-old is that pain can't be bypassed.

When Douglas Gresham, stepson to C. S. Lewis, lost his mom to cancer, he avoided talking about her, terrified by the prospect that either he or his stepfather would dissolve into tears. He believed "the most shameful thing that could happen to me would be to be reduced to tears in public."[1]

I wonder how many of us have received similar harmful messages. Suppressing grief isn't safe or honest. In the children's book *The Rabbit Listened*, something disappointing happens to Corey.[2] A series of others come along, each urging the child toward some quick fix for the problem. But when Corey doesn't feel like taking their advice by yelling, tearing down someone else's project, or pretending nothing's wrong, they each leave in a huff. That's when someone arrives who by listening guides Corey into healing, clarity, and hope. We can offer similar gifts when another is hurting. We can be present instead of rushing to repair. And it's hopeful to remember that God wants to be with us in painful and vulnerable places. Romans 8:26 says the Spirit speaks between God and us with sighs "too deep for words."

Alice Walker once said, "You think you can avoid [suffering], but actually you can't. If you do, you just get sicker, or you feel more pain. But if you can speak it, if you can write it, if you can paint it, it is very healing."[3]

Jesus Didn't Try to Solve Their Grief

When Jesus' friend Lazarus got sick, he waited to return to the city of Bethany until after Lazarus had died. He was already planning to raise him from the dead. But when he arrived, he didn't rush to solutions. He talked with Lazarus's sister Martha, engaging her what ifs about her brother; when the other sister and friends arrived, Jesus didn't berate them for not being glad Lazarus was "in a better place." He didn't chastise them for not having enough faith. He cried with them instead (John 11:35).

Jesus' goal wasn't to fix them or their grief. He let himself be moved by their pain. And he joined them in it. He didn't view their sadness as incompatible with trust in God or at odds with holiness. N. T. Wright says he wasn't putting on a show of sympathy. He was mourning the fact that death "sneers in the face of all that is lovely and beautiful."[4] If God in the flesh considers attending to grief important, we can feel the freedom, and even a holy summons, to do the same.

Diane Langberg notices that Jesus "engages human beings with the resurrection process" by inviting them to remove the stone and unbind Lazarus.[5] She contends we are invited to participate in the outworking of resurrection and renewal in our own lives and among those who are hurting around us. Some grief must be tended privately with God. But most lament needs to be brought into the light along the way with trustworthy others. That includes your community of family, friends, book club members, or fellow churchgoers. It may also sometimes involve pastors, spiritual directors, and therapists.

Sue Monk Kidd said, "When Jesus was in pain, he didn't try to squirm out of it. . . . He let it happen."[6] He sweated blood in the garden. He expressed anguish at his sense of disconnection with God from the cross. None of it made him any less divine.

For many of us, creating more capacity for hopeful lament will require work to become more comfortable with hard emotions in ourselves and others. It will mean growing beyond the tendency I showed after my grandfather's death to gloss over or suppress negative emotions. I am not alone in that impulse. Psychologist Tobin Hart calls it "spiritual bypassing" when people choose "focusing on spiritual considerations to the neglect of more basic psychological or emotional development."[7] This is not to imply that there aren't significant spiritual and theological dimensions to grief but to make it *merely* or *only* a spiritual matter is harmful.

Katherine May is convinced we need to stop acting like times of grieving, loss, or illness are "somehow silly, a failure of nerve, a lack of willpower."[8] When you or those you love enter what she calls a winter season, there are choices. You can pretend that the loss isn't as painful as it is and that everything is fine. Or you can acknowledge the cold and darkness, opening yourself to the comfort of the Spirit and of people who care for you within it.

Addictions, suicides, and other ways that sorrow can be turned inward are often connected to attempts to numb or avoid pain. It's a way that grief can become weaponized against the self or others. That may be part of why drug overdoses increased dramatically during the pandemic. US data indicates drug overdose deaths jumped a startling 30 percent in 2020.[9] This increase in what are sometimes called "deaths of despair" was extreme even amid an ongoing opioid crisis.

The truth is that grief can feel overwhelming. Some survivors say things like, "If I start crying, I will never stop," or "If I feel grief or hopelessness, I will fall into a black hole and never get out."[10] Pacing and compassion, for self and others, are essential when practicing lament.

Acknowledging grief is important; so is not staying in those places interminably or without capable and caring people to help carry the load with us. There are times when healing requires help from those with expertise in mental and emotional health. People with training in grief counseling, psychology, and pastoral ministry can help illuminate what healthy grieving looks like, see signs indicating sorrow is becoming toxic, and provide other tools to support healing and wholeness.

Suppressing Sadness

The urge to suppress grief is not a new struggle. It has always been hard to stay with lament. Job's friends were initially willing to sit with him in holy silence. Soong-Chan Rah says it was their most helpful action. He argues, "The acknowledgment that there is no human wisdom that can be offered may be our best offering to the suffering other."[11] But for Job's friends, as for many modern people intending to offer comfort, their need for answers and solutions quickly overcame their ability to remain present to his misery. Henri Nouwen contended they bypassed his cry when they started defending God and themselves. And their denial of his hard questions only exacerbated Job's despair. Nouwen warned that any "spiritual guide who anxiously avoids the painful search and nervously fills the gap created by unanswerable questions" as Job's friends did, should not be trusted.[12]

People enduring devastating losses are sometimes told God is judging their sin. That God won't give you more than you can handle. That he needed another angel in heaven.

And I've been guilty of offering simplistic solutions to suffering myself. My tendency to rush past grief didn't end when I entered adulthood. When I was in college, my youth pastor's youngest son died in a tragic accident inside the church I grew up in. Not long after, I came across an eighteenth-century poem written by a mother whose son was lost at sea. I sent the bereaved youth pastor's wife a copy with a letter that expressed my hope that she, too, would grow to a place of acceptance and trust in God. I am embarrassed by my tone of subtle reprimand that she hadn't gotten over his death. I mistook her devastation for a lack of faith.

I intended to offer hope, but I was speaking without the empathy required and into a sort of loss for which I had no context. I didn't have the wisdom to recognize the extent to which lament, and not only praise and trust, is a type of prayer that honors God, humans, and reality. This is not to say we must experience an identical loss to offer compassion or care. But it is to recognize that what is often assumed to be helpful for those who are suffering is actually cold comfort.

Kelsey Crowe and Emily McDowell encourage alternatives to unhelpful platitudes, such as texts saying you're thinking of the person who's grieving, sending a meal coupon, small gifts intended to make them smile, handling yardwork or other chores, or offering to be a point of contact for sharing updates with the community.[13] Such simple actions can be meaningful whenever you feel stuck about how to support someone through loss.

And if you're the one who's experiencing loss or grief, it's vital to be both gentle with yourself and to ask for help as you need it. After the sudden death of her father, Merissa Nathan Gerson found it was sometimes hard for her to surface awareness of her needs.[14] Her encouragement for anyone grieving is to prioritize five health essentials. Hers were sleep, water, exercise, friends, and protein. Notice how simple they are. In grief, the basics become difficult to manage. Gerson encourages anyone living with loss to memorize their five and assign them to the fingers of one hand. On hard days, you can check them off to make sure you're taking care of yourself.

Progress and the Power of Positive Thinking

Sometimes grief is painted as negativity. In the West, especially the United States, eschewing sorrow, denying suffering, and an overemphasis on positivity is commonplace. An old song by Perry Como is a great example. He crooned, "You gotta accentuate the positive, eliminate the negative, latch onto the affirmative."[15] The lyrics connect that Pollyanna perspective to biblical characters, implying that Jonah and Noah survived their ordeals because they focused on happy thoughts.

The belief in the inevitability of cultural improvement and an accompanying commitment to positivity, which Como's song tapped into, was the culmination of Enlightenment thinking. The Enlightenment was a seventeenth century network of sciences and philosophies that emphasized logic. Its proponents were captivated by the potential to triumph over the physical world, tradition, and human nature itself, hinted at by inventions like the telescope and microscope.

A sense of possessing the ability to unlock the mysteries of the universe abounded. Water could be clean, diseases cured, and the stars scrutinized more fully. There's no question there were advances to celebrate. And it isn't surprising such things sparked new emphases of reason, progress, and science and fading attention for tradition and religion. The so-called modern world that was the outworking of Enlightenment thinking was characterized by capitalism, industrialized military power, and automation of basic means of production. Many enthused modernity had "swept us away from all traditional types of social order."[16] Commitment to progress took on an almost religious fervor for many and was sometimes even overtly preached from pulpits.

The American version of faith in progress has dominated a lot of our history. Puritan John Winthrop preached America was meant to be "a city on a hill" from aboard a ship headed to Boston in 1630.[17] Many political leaders adopted that kind of religious imagery, proclaiming the United States was living into its manifest destiny of a divinely appointed expansion of territory and political power from sea to shining sea.

These things reached new heights in the twentieth century. Commitment to progress was combined with magical thinking about the power of an optimistic outlook and a view of sorrow and grief as pessimistic and self-fulfilling. A key figure in all this was Norman Vincent Peale, the famous Manhattan preacher and author of *The Power of Positive Thinking*. It was an immediate success when it was published in 1952, and spent 186 weeks on the *New York Times* bestseller list, sold around five million copies, and was translated into fourteen languages.[18]

In 1954, the founding publisher of both *Time* and *Fortune* magazines wrote, "The business of America is to progress; and Progress is the business of America. We are a nation forever on the march."[19]

Trouble in Paradise

By the late twentieth century, it seemed like he was right. The future looked bright as the Cold War came to a surprising and abrupt end. Francis Fukuyama declared that ghosts from past conflicts could finally be laid to rest and a new era of justice, freedom, and dignity were on the horizon.[20] He called it the end of history.

But experience soon tempered his optimism. The Bosnian war followed the breakup of Yugoslavia and with it came revelations of ethnic cleansing. Marija Koprivnjak wrote "Jeremianic Lamentations over Bosnia and Herzegovina" during the war. She asked who "will stop your war-fire and destruction" and "who will heal the countless broken hearts?"—even as her lament acknowledged there were no answers for such questions.[21] Two former Serbian leaders were ultimately charged with genocide and others with war crimes.[22]

Then was the carnage in Littleton, Colorado, when two students entered their high school dressed in trench coats carrying duffle bags of guns and killed fifteen people, including themselves.[23] At the time, it was the deadliest school shooting in history. The countless mass shootings since are tragic reminders of the kind of havoc the pain of a few broken people with access to assault weapons can unleash.

And then the 9/11 attacks happened. Almost three thousand people died in the Twin Towers and on United Airlines Flight 93 after passengers crash-landed the plane before terrorists could attack another target.[24] Most Americans had no idea just how much (or why) we were hated in some parts of the world. Two decades of war with Iraq and Afghanistan followed.

The financial crisis of 2008 and the great recession which followed it led to catastrophic loss in home values and widespread unemployment. Two trillion dollars in growth were lost globally.[25] Incomes and prospects in the United States started shrinking for the first time since World War II, and the middle class has continued to dwindle.[26] Young people were disproportionately impacted.[27]

These things made it difficult to maintain the idea of a world getting steadily better. We were inundated with new reasons to grieve, including unprecedented violence on US soil, but acknowledging the fear and sorrow felt too unsettling for many. Instead of entering the hard and necessary work of lament, many resisted grief. It was often channeled into anger or the pursuit of retribution because those things fit with American values like capability, optimism, and proactivity. For some, it all inspired a scarcity mindset and a search for scapegoats—immigrants, millennials, terrorists, and opponents' political parties are all groups held responsible for the sorry state of things.

Former President Trump served as a flashpoint for desires of a return to an idealized past with clear ideas of greatness and success. It is no coincidence that he and his family were fans of the man who wrote *The Power of Positive Thinking*, often attending services at his church. Peale even officiated Trump's first wedding in 1977. Trump said, "When Peale preached, [I] never wanted to leave the church."[28]

And it's not hard to trace his influence on Trump's apparently boundless confidence. Peale exhorted people to stamp "indelibly on your mind a mental picture of yourself as succeeding . . . hold this picture tenaciously . . . [and maintain it] no matter how badly things seem to be going at the moment."[29]

His other guidelines include rejecting fear, never thinking of yourself as failing, and intentionally inflating your view of your abilities.[30] Whatever else may be said about his impact on political discourse during his administration and beyond, Trump is nothing if not a modern disciple of Peale.

Grief Suppressed

But when mourning is resisted individually or corporately, it usually comes out sideways, sometimes violently. And so, alongside growing nostalgia for radical positivity, more anger and reactivity were also brewing. As greater numbers flocked to social media—joining their digital forebears in the dubious ability to comment on strangers' posts and connect with old friends and friends of friends, with complex algorithms humming behind the scenes—the impulse to treat fellow humans with kindness and dignity seemed compromised. Online communication started being flooded with contempt and cruelty. And it wasn't just strangers and bots: family, friends, and colleagues were at odds with one another.

Part of the issue has to do with social media technologies themselves. Karen Hao says, "Machine-learning models that maximize engagement also favor controversy, misinformation, and extremism."[31] Social media companies track users' opinions, the content they engage, and how their viewpoints change as a result. Regardless of the issue, the models learn to feed users' increasingly extreme viewpoints and "they measurably become more polarized" over time.[32]

In other words, the more Facebook and other social media forms succeed under current models, the more divided we become. The sense of increased embattlement is not a figment of our collective imagination. And while those amassing power and wealth through social media companies with harmful practices should be held accountable (and we should participate in such media with caution), there's more to it.

Zygmunt Bauman famously observed that modern tendencies to equate logic and progress with good were exposed as myth by the highly logical industrial scale of the Holocaust.[33] Before his death in 2017, he contended social networks are poor substitutes for real community. He argued social media often discourages dialogue because "it is so easy to avoid controversy," prioritizing connection with those who agree with us.[34]

Our invitation is to allow a misguided conviction in progress and demands for counterfeit positivity to be put to rest. I wonder what would happen if we cultivated more curiosity toward those unlike ourselves, resisting self-congratulatory echo chambers, simplistic readings of inflammatory headlines, and marketing and media that profit from division. It might free us from living in denial, focused on either how right we are or fighting enemies. What if we had more actual conversations and really listened instead of waiting for our turn to speak? Philosopher Merold Westphal advocates looking for areas of shared concerns and values with those who aren't like us. He says that has the potential to make us less inclined to "language that seeks to denigrate, manipulate, or seduce our opponents" as well as literal violence.[35] Instead of blame or denial, we might embrace more humility, compassion, and the welcome of both neighbors and strangers, which could free us to grieve and seek repair when those things haven't happened.

Not Around but Through

Soong-Chan Rah points out that cultures that focus on victory and resist engaging suffering, make the mistake of allowing praise to replace lament. He argues that without lament, praise becomes hollow; he contends that neither refusing to comfort someone who is hurting nor attempting "to diffuse and minimize the emotional response of lament serves the suffering other. It only adds to the suffering."[36] That's why we're invited to weep with those who weep instead of pressing them to reaffirm their faith quickly and cheerfully (Romans 12:15).

A few years ago, I read a reflection on lament that offered several suggestions for practices including tearing cloth. Something clicked for me. There was a rightness in the idea of enacting something I'd read about biblical figures engaging. I started keeping bits of cloth on hand when I did my morning prayers and as I read the news. When I heard about another shooting or a catastrophic storm or fire or earthquake, it became a way to pray with my hands, providing a visceral outlet to express my grief, anger, or powerlessness at the suffering of others.

At first, I engaged this way of praying on my own, but as I shared it with close friends and online, the idea resonated. I also started noticing that people I hosted in spiritual direction conversations were coming with more grief, anxiety, and complex losses than had been true in previous seasons. Spiritual direction isn't coaching or counseling, but contemplative listening to help another tune into the Holy and their own truest self. I was listening with those who were processing childhood abuse, church hurts, illnesses, and adoption traumas. When I suggested the possibility of framing their experiences as holy invitations to lament, I consistently witnessed resonance and relief. But for the majority, this was quickly followed by the confession that they didn't really know *how* to lament.

When my family's hearts were healing following a loss, Torey and her dad talked a lot about "not wasting the pain." They didn't mean powering through grief or jumping through psychological or theological hoops to argue that a devastating tragedy was somehow good. They were describing a hope that on the other side of holy, hard, intentional grieving would be restoration. Psychologists talk about that potential as "posttraumatic growth." It's the experience of emotional development following a struggle that is "not simply a return to baseline [but] the experience of improvement" that can be life changing.[37]

That's what Paul was talking about when he wrote that one of the reasons God comforts us when we are in pain is so that we can be a source of consolation for others who are suffering (2 Corinthians 1:3-7). The Spirit is faithful to offer us comfort when we suffer. And it's also true that enduring suffering and loss is also meant to overflow into more empathy, compassion, and kindness for others. On the other side of loss, we comfort others with consolations like those we've received.

After losing his beloved wife, C. S. Lewis initially told himself, "Love is not the whole of a man's life. I was happy before I ever met H. . . . People get over these things."[38] Then he'd find himself dissolving into tears, anguish, and anger.

The 1993 film *Shadowlands* tells the story of his late-in-life romance and the subsequent loss of his wife to cancer. The beloved author lost his mother when he was an adolescent, so he was no stranger to grief. Early in the film, he is depicted speaking in packed lecture halls saying things like, "Pain is God's megaphone to rouse a deaf world," and "The blows of his chisel that hurt us so much are what make us perfect."[39] It's not so much that those perspectives are wrong. But they are profoundly incomplete.

The film exposes how such sentiments can ring hollow in the face of real suffering. Lewis's story offers a powerful corrective to tendencies to rush toward pat theological-sounding truisms.

It is essential to have the courage to allow yourself to be changed by loss. It honors the love implicit in it.

When you live through suffering, life will indeed go on. Sometimes that will feel like a good thing and at others it may seem like the worst thing possible. As you move through healing, it will vary day by day and sometimes even minute by minute. My hope is that you will sense that you are known, held, and guided by Love. Rediscovering the practice of lament together can unlock ways to let ourselves fully experience grief as it is, in an unhurried and intuitive pace.

Tearing Practice

In Scripture, when King David learned that his friend, Jonathan, had been killed in battle, he expressed his loss viscerally. When Tamar was tricked and betrayed, she let her grief be seen and heard. When Job lost everything, his response was embodied. They tore clothing, let themselves cry, fasted from meals, and wore ashes.

For this practice, gather paper or cloth for tearing. This doesn't have to be complicated! Junk mail, old shopping lists, and magazines all work well. Old T-shirts, cleaning rags, or bandannas are also great. Natural fibers are usually easiest to tear. If the cloth has a hem, trim it off and cut notches to get your tearing started.

Consider what you want to practice lamenting today. What happened? Who was involved? What did you hear or feel or see? Focus on your emotions as you hold the paper or cloth in open palms.

When you are ready to express your sadness, begin tearing. Listen to the sounds. Touch the frayed edges. Tear as many or as few strips as you like. The pieces can be large or as tiny as confetti. Hold the torn pieces in your hands, noticing how they reflect the brokenness you're lamenting. Allow this to be prayer. If at any point you feel overwhelmed, stop and take slow, deep breaths.

Then imagine releasing any pain or disappointment and receiving comfort and healing. What was it like to tear the paper or cloth? You might have experienced sadness, anxiety, or anger. You might have noticed memories of other losses emerging alongside the one you initially focused on. All of this is welcome. It might be helpful to journal about your experience or share it with a trusted friend or two.

You might throw the frayed strips in a trash or compost bin to release them. You might continue processing what you're letting go of and what you're carrying forward by braiding or twisting the strips together and tying them on your wrist or carrying them in your pocket for a time before you let them go. You could bury the strips to signify a hope for renewal, adding some flower seeds or other seeds if you choose.

Tearing Practice for Children and Families

You can engage a similar tearing activity with children. Gather paper or cloth for tearing.

Invite everyone participating to consider a worry or loss. Encourage them to listen to their hearts and to each other about it.

What or who have they missed? What has been scary? What has been hard?

Invite them to tell the story of those feelings with their hands, encouraging them to tear their paper or cloth into strips.

They can tear as much or as little as they want. Each person can decide how thick or thin they want their strips to be. Invite them to let their mad or sad feelings talk to them as they tear. Encourage them to listen to the sound the paper makes and touch the rough edges. Let them know that they are welcome to ask God to be with them in their feelings.

When everyone has finished tearing as much as they'd like, talk about the activity together.

Ask questions like,

What was it like to tear your paper?

What did your heart feel?

How did that feel in your body?

If you asked God to be with you in your feelings, what did you notice?

3

Learning to Speak Sadness

Tell me about despair, yours,
and I will tell you mine.

MARY OLIVER

ABOUT EIGHTEEN MONTHS BEFORE OUR FIRE, Torey called from a friend's house late one night. It was just before Thanksgiving. After a brief phone call with an ex-boyfriend, who seemed intoxicated, he had texted her a series of violent threats. Thankfully, she wasn't alone. Two friends were with her, but she was stunned and perplexed about how to respond.

Her dad drove to College Station to be with her and accompany her to the police station to file a report. For the rest of the semester, she was told never to walk alone. It was a scary way to end her first semester of college. We all breathed a sigh of relief when exams were over and she could head home for Christmas.

But a few days later, Bernie Madoff was arrested for securities fraud after confessing to his sons that the asset management unit of the family business was a colossal Ponzi scheme. Since my husband's company had a small investment with Madoff, revelations of the fraud unleashed havoc in his office. There were FBI searches, arrests, and seizures of property. Initially, many among law enforcement and the public assumed investors were participating in the conspiracy.

Even after it turned out that couldn't be further from the truth, several men from the company that owned Kyle's used the confusion to their advantage, seeing to it that he and many colleagues lost their jobs in disgrace while funneling cash to their accounts. Kyle was harassed and portrayed as a criminal. He'd been on the edge of being able to retire early and had dreams of giving more generously to causes he believed in and traveling to do relief work and community service in his freer time. Those dreams were dashed. He was devastated—we all were.

Worse, our marriage was strained after years of leading the church we'd help plant. We were burned-out and distant, having spent more than we had to give on our community for too many years. We had encouraged others to take regular sabbaths and sabbaticals but failed to do so ourselves. So when we needed each other most, we found we barely knew each other, separated by the good work we'd both been doing and by unresolved conflicts that had built up over time.

Not the Most Wonderful Time of the Year

Earlier that fall, we'd made plans to host my extended family and some of their family for Christmas. I'd been planning for months, going all out to make it an extra festive time. I bought enough holiday china so we could serve the meals on real dishes. I covered several folding tables with white tablecloths to create a single long table to host our many guests. I created place cards out of clear glass ornaments I'd decorated with ribbon matching the dishes and stuffed with cardstock onto which I'd carefully penned each person's name. I even had T-shirts made with all our names printed on the back. I think acting the role of superhostess was a way of distracting myself from all that was starting to feel off-track in our lives.

And since I didn't know how to be anything except that version of strong, we didn't change our plans after Torey was threatened and Kyle's career was upended. As everyone gathered for the holiday, we told everyone as little as possible and powered through. Kyle was often gone for calls and meetings to address the mounting crisis, but since that wasn't unusual with his demanding business and ministry schedule, few understood what was actually happening.

Behind closed doors, Kyle was despondent and openly grieving. I was torn between wanting to support him and my own pain at feeling abandoned by him (and, if I'm honest, God) not long before. I had desperately needed help and my requests for support had gone ignored. The complexity was heightened by my need to mother our daughter well after her traumatic experience, my duty to our church, and a sense of obligation to make Christmas magical for everyone.

I was hospitable and smiling on the surface but numb inside. I didn't know who to ask for help. On one of countless trips to the grocery store that season, I heard Sufjan Stevens's melancholy carol "That was the worst Christmas ever!" for the first time. It tells the story of an awful Christmas from his childhood. The scene he paints couldn't have been more different from my own, yet his song gave voice to my confusion and grief during what I believed was supposed to be the most wonderful time of the year.

Like many laments, Sufjan's doesn't have a neatly resolved happy ending. The last words, "Silent night, nothing feels right," give way to a lonely lilting tune hummed by two singers. As the instruments fade, a single voice sings the final notes. The sound is sad, a minor chord. And yet, somehow, there is also hope and courage in the fading tune. It's the power of telling the truth about something difficult without whitewashing. It's the permission to say things aren't as they should be or even as they might seem. I didn't realize at the time that Sufjan's song is a sort of prayer, because it was unlike any prayers I'd been taught to pray.

One gift we receive from the artists among us is finding fresh ways of articulating grief, as Sufjan's song did for me. I love the way Alynda Segarra, of the band Hurray for the Riff Raff, describes the prophetic courage artists can demonstrate. She says her job as an artist is facing hard truths and uncertain futures without giving anyone "false hopes that this isn't happening, and that everything's gonna be cozy."[1]

In that season, other songs and prayers of lament were waiting for me, in the Psalms, in the Prophets, and beyond. These narratives are filled with injustice and violence and pain. No rush to faith and hope. No pat answers involving something about trust or sovereignty. Just the raw, unvarnished reality of brokenness and suffering. And a cry—spoken or unspoken—for God's intervention. As Old Testament theologian Walter Brueggemann knows, "The Psalms have what power they have for us because we know life to be like that.

In a society that engages in great denial and grows numb by avoidance," we need songs and stories that tell the truth about life.[2]

When I listen to Sufjan's song today, it still moves me to tears as it did all those years ago. But now the tears are less a stirring of unhealed wounds and more a shimmer of empathy for the people we each were when we lived through those days. And gratitude for the grace that has flowed from that season when the Spirit first began to teach me the healing power of lament.

Crying for Help

Lament can be words spoken, written, or sung. It can also be postures or actions that give expression to pain. Some laments, like Sufjan's, simply and profoundly tell the story of loss and grief. And that is an important starting point. We need to know we are welcome to tell the truth to ourselves, God, and others about pain and anger. We need to share our own stories and to cultivate resilience for hearing the stories of others. Lament is not being negative, depressing, or "too much." And when suffering is kept in the dark, the weight of unresolved sorrow remains like a cancer, and harmful secrets are encouraged.

Mark Vroegop started learning to lament after the tragic death of his child only days before his due date. He says:

> Lament is how we bring our sorrow to God. Without lament we won't know how to process pain. Silence, bitterness, and even anger can dominate our spiritual lives instead. Without lament we won't know how to help people walking through sorrow. Instead, we'll offer trite solutions, unhelpful comments, or impatient responses.

> What's more, without this sacred song of sorrow, we'll miss the lessons historic laments are intended to teach us.[3]

Laments can include, as the psalmists often did, a cry for divine help or relief. Michael Card paints it as, "The stumbling, exhausted, world-weary place where suffering and God meet."[4]

As we learn to make more room for lament, we are also invited to create freedom for young people to express pain and sorrow when they need to. Modeling hopeful lament for them in age-appropriate ways is a crucial part of this. It's also important to make time to listen with them about the full range of their emotions, difficult and otherwise.

In her children's book, *Crying Is Like the Rain*, Heather Hawk Feinberg writes about how some people get worried or scared by crying, or try to hush it up by being silly. Feinberg argues that "all feelings have a purpose" and instead of fearing hard emotions, we can see them as inner storms.[5] She encourages engaging kids in a game of doing a "weather report" of their feelings, helping them welcome their emotional weather as it is, without trying to change it.

The Power of Music

The hopeful news is that we haven't utterly forgotten the power of lament, even if some of us rarely call it by that name. We listen to sad music or watch movies telling stories of pain and loss when we're sad, not to make ourselves more unhappy but intuitively knowing they are ways of expressing our grief. Psychologists Liila Taruffi and Stefan Koelsch found that listening to sad music helps people process memories, regulate negative moods, and activate empathy.[6]

In *Harry Potter and the Half-Blood Prince*, Fawkes the Phoenix sings a lament after Dumbledore's death.[7] It is a mournful, otherworldly tune, but Harry and his friends somehow feel better after listening to it. The song has no words—it doesn't need them. The notes tell the story of a great and good man lost to their world. It expresses who Dumbledore was, how his life was spent, and what his example invites those who remain to do and be. Similarly, when Gandalf is lost in *The Fellowship of the Ring*, the elves sing a lament for him. Its stanzas celebrate a life well-lived and wonder what the world will be without him. When the others ask Legolas to translate, he demurs, saying for him "the grief was still too near, a matter for tears and not yet for song."[8]

When David learned that Saul and Jonathan had died in battle, the man after God's heart sang a dirge for them. He also instructed the song be recorded and taught to the people of Judah as a way of remembering their lives (2 Samuel 1:18). Traditional laments often took the form of songs sung for the dead, frequently by women. The Hebrew word for a lament song (קין [*qyn*]) is related to a root that refers to a female singer and alludes to striking an instrument and singing to its tune.[9]

In the African American church, spirituals have filled a similar role of grieving and finding hope to begin again in community. James H. Cone's powerful work *The Cross and the Lynching Tree* traces the horrific history of lynching in the United States and the ways that music was a balm for weary Black souls living amid such evils. He highlights parallels with Jesus' tortured death on the cross and the violence and degradation of lynching, in that "both are symbols of death [yet] one represents a message of hope and salvation, while the other signifies the negation of that message by white supremacy."[10]

Cone's text is suffused with song lyrics, including familiar tunes like "Nobody Knows the Trouble I See" and "Strange Fruit." The first verse of "Strange Fruit" goes, "Southern trees bear strange fruit/Blood on the leaves and blood at the root/ Black body swinging in the Southern breeze/Strange fruit hanging from the poplar trees."[11]

Cone asserts that songs like those sung in churches and by blues singers helped lift the oppressed in the Jim Crow era "above their troubles by offering them an opportunity to experience 'love and loss' as a liberating catharsis."[12] Maya Angelou believed people survived slavery, segregation, and other racial injustices "because they were able to write of their despair and even of their hope in their songs. They were able to preach of dismay and dreams in their sermons."[13]

A Brief and Incomplete History of Lament

Honest, faithful lament can be expressed in all kinds of embodied ways. In the Bible, lament was sometimes enacted by sprinkling dust or ashes on the body (Esther 4:1), cutting or plucking hair (Nehemiah 13:25), or tearing garments (Job 1:20; 2:12). It could take the form of tears, wailing aloud, wearing rough clothing (Psalm 35:13), removing jewelry (Exodus 33:4), neglecting personal hygiene (Matthew 6:16-17), physically covering the mouth (Micah 3:7), or remaining in wordless silence and fasting (Judges 20:26). Grief could be expressed by leaving the head uncovered, lying on the ground (2 Samuel 13:31), covering the head or face, going barefoot (Isaiah 20:2), placing hands on the head (Jeremiah 2:37), or wearing special mourning garments (Genesis 38:14).

An Egyptian limestone carving from the late eighteenth or early nineteenth century BCE depicts mourners. Some "kneel on the ground sorrowfully holding their heads in their hands" while another "bends over to touch the ground, perhaps gathering dust to throw over her head" as others hide their faces behind their hands.[14] Another holds his head, which is thrown back in dismay, in his hands. Wine and food, either as an offering for the dead or for a funeral meal for the mourners (or both) is also represented. These expressions of grief seem oddly familiar. I shouldn't be surprised since suffering is part of the human experience. Embodied expressions of loss transcend time and culture. The Bible and other sacred texts and artifacts preserve a rich and varied memory of the ways sorrow can be released.

In the ancient world, periods of mourning after death could last weeks or even months. After Jacob's death, for example, he was mourned for thirty days as his body was prepared for burial. The Egyptians, honoring the father of the man who had helped preserve their lives through the famine, continued grieving his death an additional forty days and traveled with Joseph's family to Canaan to his burial. In Canaan, "they held there a very great and sorrowful lamentation; and he observed a time of mourning for his father seven days" (Genesis 50:10). Their sorrow was so acute, residents renamed the spot because of it. They called it *Abel-mizraim*, the mourning of Egypt (Genesis 50:11).

In some cultures, the death of a beloved, prayers for deliverance, and other losses were marked by the mourners cutting their own flesh. It's important to say that this is a form of lament God discourages (Leviticus 19:28; 21:5). I'm convinced that's because it is a type of grieving that further harms the mourner. Such actions would only serve to add more pain and anguish to those who are already suffering. Other mourning practices tell the story of brokenness without contributing to more suffering. A torn garment can be mended, hair cut off can grow again, a body dusted with ashes or dirt can be washed. While pain and losses must be acknowledged in real and significant ways, life is to be treasured and embraced even in seasons of pain.

In our day, this ancient impulse to give voice to suffering by practicing self-harm is being revealed anew for some, particularly among young women and girls. But like abusing drugs or alcohol to numb pain, this practice only creates greater damage. This book cannot take the place of therapy or crisis intervention. But my hope is that it will provide tools and permission to bring pain and grief into the light so that it doesn't turn into more harm.

In the past, mourners were sometimes hired "to give by their loud lamentation the external tokens of sorrow" (2 Chronicles 35:25; Jeremiah 9:17).[15] The people playing instruments and "making a commotion" outside Jairus's home after the death of his daughter, which once perplexed me, were such mourners (Matthew 9:23). In ancient Egypt, mourner was one of the few professional occupations available to women.[16] These women were referred to as *dryt*, "mourners," who at times played the important roles of impersonating Isis and Nephthys, goddesses who mourned the death of Osiris—"The god of the afterlife with whom a deceased person was identified."[17]

Dryt wore special hairstyles and clothing to mark their status and were expected to make "an ostentatious display of grief which included loud wailing [and] . . . smearing the body with dirt and tearing at dishevelled [*sic*] hair" as ways of expressing profound sorrow.[18] What might shift among us if we were more willing to speak of and engage grief in visceral ways, less concerned with appearing dignified or controlled?

Modern professional mourners are also called *moirologists* from the Greek words for fate (*moira*) and speech (*logos*). They "see their work as helping the family grieve and accompanying the deceased in their journey to the afterlife" with improvised songs that tell the stories of lost loved ones.[19] The tradition has roots in Greek tragedies when a singer would begin a dirge and the chorus would join.

My friend who enjoys Korean language dramas with her husband, told me that the presence of professional mourners is a frequent occurrence in them. In Asia, they date back at least two millennia to the Han dynasty, though they were banned temporarily in China during the Cultural Revolution. A modern-day mourner named Hu Xinglian is "famous for her *kusang*, which literally means crying and shouting."[20] At one funeral, she and the rest of her company joined a family wearing white, the traditional color of mourning in China, and after a communal meal, she voiced a wailing eulogy into a microphone, crawling toward the deceased's coffin as his family stood weeping.[21] She said these demonstrations are meant to convey the depth of love for the deceased and the pain their death brings.

In Kenya, practices like these have been taken up by younger generations. A professional mourner in his early twenties named Daniel Ochieng maintains his work of mourning is "a talent like singing."[22] Zakes Mda's novel *Ways of Dying* tells the story of Toloki who travels from funeral to funeral in South Africa as a professional mourner, hoping to offer comfort to those impacted by poverty, racism, and violence. He wears black clothing, a top hat, and a "sacred fragrance" as "a hallmark of his profession" and wails at the gravesides of families who pay a fee for his services.[23]

While rarer in the West, professional mourners do exist. The 1966 spy film *Funeral in Berlin* starring Michael Caine featured a trained mourner.[24] And, Hank Williams's "Nobody's Lonesome for Me" includes the line "When the time comes around for me to lay down and die, I bet I'll have to go and hire me someone to cry."[25] A professional mourner in London described his job as helping people process their grief, which practitioners like himself are well-equipped to do by much practice and "also because our heads *aren't* clouded by grief."[26]

I don't have plans to hire mourners, but I have come to think quite differently about their existence. In the past, it seemed grossly performative or evidence of a morbid fascination with death and suffering. But now I'm convinced they're reminders that grief is real, important, and taxing. They model the importance of expressing sadness. They demonstrate how vital it is to let grief be articulated and heard. Historic and modern mourners highlight the reality that suffering sometimes invites us into community, and at times includes practitioners who can journey with us for a season with compassion and experiential wisdom. And that it's okay to need help with the hard work of grief.

Psalm-Writing Practice

To write your own song or poem of lament, you don't need any special skills. The finished work doesn't have to be good. It is more about the process than the product.

Start with bringing to mind what you need to lament today. It can be something systemic. It might be something small but significant. It can be a loss or sorrow from the past or something going on right now.

Take a moment to decide what you want to focus on, noticing what happened. Who was involved? What did you hear or feel or see? Hold this memory in your mind.

Take a few minutes to journal a little about what you want to grieve. As much as you're able, try not to censor your thoughts. As one person I host in direction described it, let your words rest on the page. You can lay them down there without needing to be clear or concise for now.

To create your own psalm, use your journaling as a basis for writing your own song of mourning and release. You might begin with calling out to the Helper. You could use a favorite name for God or a description like *shepherd*, *healer*, or *loving parent.* Next, try briefly naming the help you need. Then, put language around what you're grieving. Be as specific as you can. You could use questioning words as the psalmists often do, like *why*, *how long*, and *when* (see Psalm 13:1; 44:24; 119:82).

You could include your belief in God's coming deliverance or remember times of past goodness at this point in your psalm if you'd like. Then, describe what help you're asking for in more detail. Consider closing your psalm with your hope of being able to thank God for relief and renewal in the future.

You might try reading your song aloud. You could even sing it to the tune of a favorite song.

Song-Writing Practice for Children and Families

Invite children to write their own song, poem, or psalm by writing (or having a grown up transcribe) their *why*, *how long*, and *when* questions for God. Have them read their psalms aloud or have a grown up do so. Wonder together what God thinks about their poem or song.

You could also try singing their words together to the tune of a familiar song like "Over the Rainbow," "Mary Had a Little Lamb," or "Let It Go."

4

Letting Sorrow Be a Conversation with God

You have kept count of my tossings;
put my tears in your bottle.
Are they not in your record?

PSALM 56:8

WHEN I ENROLLED IN SEMINARY, it couldn't have been a bigger surprise. Torey had just gotten her master's degree, and my husband and I witnessed her joy-filled wedding and were thrilled she was building a life with the wonderful man she married. And me? I had already completed a graduate degree more than a decade prior. Not to mention I'd spent most of my adult life serving the church.

But I had been changed by my family's season of upheaval. We all had. The losses required something from us. We couldn't just move forward as if nothing had happened. We each had help getting through that time from friends, family, and counselors. I found my first spiritual director during those days of recovery. As I moved toward putting the pieces of my life and faith back together, it became clear God was inviting me to offer that same gift of compassionate listening to others, hosting them in spiritual conversations about joy, hope, love, and loss.

Lament is about lost or forgotten love. It is the dream of resurrection. Lament dares to believe God is interested in our pain and loss. It trusts God is moved by suffering. It is engaging grief with confidence that God doesn't turn a blind eye to cruelty, greed, oppression, or deceit. It is practicing the hope that God truly is near to the brokenhearted.

The Psalms and Prophets are all about connection with God. But not just any connection: Walter Brueggemann says, "Israel insists that the communion be honest, open to criticism, and capable of transformation. These are the prayers of a people with a deep memory of liberation and a profound hope for a new kingdom."[1] He contends our culture is addicted to denial and that laments "provide a way for healing candor."[2] Lament, and not just hope and celebration, need to be welcome in our lives.

Laments aren't a rejection of faith but an embrace of a faith that loves justice and mercy. It's an invitation to bring our whole selves, families, and communities, with all their complexities, into God's loving presence. Lament creates a chance for something new to be born because it acknowledges what is missing. I am convinced it is our best hope for healing the divisions that plague us. We have some unlearning and relearning to do together. We need to rediscover our history and get creative about new ways to engage grief and confession.

Brueggemann says psalms of praise and thanksgiving are only partial forms on their own. They admit trouble exists, implying a need for deliverance. That perspective is also evident in the hope of deliverance in Isaiah 61, which inspired Jesus' first sermon in his hometown. Isaiah said he'd been sent to bring good news to the oppressed, hope for the brokenhearted, and liberty for captives. He was offering comfort for anyone in sorrow. He was bringing them a garland to replace the ashes of mourning.

If oppression didn't exist, there would be no need for those kinds of proclamations. But cruelty and evil happened in Israel just as they do among us today. The prophet declared that because their shame was doubled, their restoration would be too.

Grief in Action

Lament can also be actions that shed light on loss or injustice. Tearing garments, throwing ashes, and holding silence enact the brokenness of suffering. Such things give an outlet for expressing pain instead of stuffing it. The ancient world was full of such prophetic actions, which are a call for deliverance in times of suffering. Those kinds of laments are sometimes humans crying out to God. And other times they're God communicating with people.

Isaiah wore sackcloth to convey his mourning for Israel's coming judgment, and walked around naked for three years to indicate the humiliating way the Egyptians and Cushites would be enslaved by the Assyrians, demonstrating that God considers strangers and former oppressors worthy of compassion

(Isaiah 20:3-6). Jeremiah once took a terra cotta jug and led elders and priests to the valley of Hinnom. After pronouncing judgment on their child sacrifice, he broke the jug: God was going to break them and their city in a way that couldn't be mended. He said the days were coming when the valley be renamed Place of Slaughter (Jeremiah 19).

As we face frequent mass shootings and other violence around the world, political and cultural division, and environmental disasters, I wonder what prophetic lament might inspire renewal and redemptive movements among us. The prophets revealed ritualized demonstrations and everyday actions can be imbued with meaning—they have the power to communicate grief and hope; they can display love and the possibility of redemption, honoring the reality of loss while refusing to surrender to futility. I'm not suggesting anyone stroll naked around town, but I think we can take some cues from the prophets. Their actions transcend words and are the kind of lament that can spark healing.

A person I host in spiritual direction once described a Lenten practice of engaging in an "indignant fast" after enduring numerous difficulties and losses. She understood she was welcome to bring her complaint before God. Her actions were an embodied prayer asking the Holy One, as many psalms do, "How long, O Lord?" Marches, taking a knee, and other forms of nonviolent protest are other modern forms of prophetic lament.

You might write a litany or play about what you are grieving and ask your family, book club, or worship community to do a reading of it with you. You can incorporate renewal, hope for the future, and areas of posttraumatic growth, or you can choose to end the story in a minor key, at least for now. You could even provide noisemakers like those often used in the Jewish celebration of Purim. For Purim, they're shaken whenever Haman's name is spoken. You could shake noisemakers whenever your play's villain—anything from cancer to divorce to death—is mentioned.

You could write a song of lament and sing it to the tune of a familiar hymn or other song. Nancy Lee describes the creative adaptation and inspiration of using biblical dirges and laments by "peoples of local cultures, influenced by the sacred texts, yet developing distinctive expressions shaped by the needs and practices of their communities."[3] Songs of lament have the power to articulate both mourning and the strength to endure. Poetry can similarly articulate love and loss when the particular sheds light on the universal. Such words, spoken or sung, share an ability to shape-shift, meeting us where we are. Their power to move us into more grace and love cannot be overestimated.

Sometimes Sorrow Whispers and Sometimes It Shouts

Lament is a kind of holy speech, uttered to and before God. It is sometimes whispered quietly, in solitude. Other times, it has to be shouted in community. Any of that can be worship that begs for God's mercy, faithfulness, and goodness, because worship is engaging the mystery of an unseen God—honoring divine goodness and hoping for grace and mercy in time of need. Worship is about relating with the Holy. It's acknowledging people and creation were made good alongside naming anything that gets in the way of that original goodness.

Lament can announce where justice is lacking. Richard Foster wrote of the witness of the spiritual leader of the Azusa Street Revival: "Seymour understood clearly the implications of glossolalia for interracial reconciliation and community. This he saw in ways that [a white colleague] and many of the other white leaders *never* saw."[4] Foster said it makes sense that a child of slaves who lived in a time and place plagued with rampant KKK violence would be well-suited to recognize "Pentecost as a new Jubilee requiring the release of the broken and the bruised from their oppression."[5]

In 1906, Seymour celebrated that many nationalities were worshiping together, saying they'd been "made one lump, one bread, all one body in Christ Jesus. There is no Jew or Gentile, bond or free [among us]."[6] In the beginning, white pastors were drawn to the movement, confessing their racism and joyfully partnering with Seymour. But early promise was eclipsed as old patterns of segregation in worship reestablished themselves.

More recent movements have also failed to achieve genuine reconciliation, even in the church. I remember the fierce competition among denominations in my hometown and the extent to which they stayed racially segregated. I grew up in a denomination founded to preserve racial segregation without knowing it. Osheta Moore says, "The racial reconciliation movement of the 1980s and '90s that the American church bought wholesale emphasized a unity without sacrificial Christlike love."[7] Claiming to not see color was inadequate for healing division because it was too interested in staying calm, collected, and, above all, *nice*. It ignored the admonition for sinners, especially the rich and powerful, to purify their hearts through holy lament (James 5:1-6).

This is not to imply that nowhere in the United States, church or otherwise, is there evidence of movement toward the promise of liberty and the pursuit of happiness. But it is to notice that we have often failed to live into that promise for African Americans, Asian Americans, Latinos, immigrants, indigenous peoples, women, and others. Our moment in time is one that invites lament—over hateful speech and actions and their enduring consequences—when repentance and restoration haven't happened. We need genuine peacemaking. And we need to know that peacemaking is not the same as peacekeeping.

Abraham Lincoln understood the need to engage lament among a diverse people. In the second year of the civil war, he called for a day of fasting and prayer. He wrote that we'd forgotten God's goodness, assuming "all these blessings were produced by some superior wisdom and virtue of our own."[8] It was only right, he said, to humble ourselves and pray for forgiveness. What might happen if modern leaders embraced a posture of confession instead of accusation and called communities to seek God's mercy?

Lament Is Honesty with Ourselves and God

Lament demands honesty. Faithful sorrow can provide solace while waiting for hope's return. It can sustain life and joy when healing is incomplete or even when it never comes. Margaret Guenther once met a woman in a nursing home who refused to be honest about how furious she was with God about her illness.

She "spent her last months filled equally with rage and cancer. Her rigid piety made it impossible for her to question God's purpose, let alone express anger."[9] She was polite to her visitors but made life hell for the poorly paid women who cared for her.

This woman hurt herself and others. She forfeited a peaceful death. She saved face with a counterfeit holiness which concealed violence toward herself and her caretakers. She missed the chance to be comforted by the Spirit who draws near to the brokenhearted.

My friend Darcy Hansen's doctoral research focuses on grief and loss. It inspired her to create a course on finding life through sorrow. Using storytelling, art, and poetry, her students talked about death and other types of losses. She taught them the ancient spiritual practice of *memento mori*, Latin for "remember you will die." *Memento mori* is an invitation to treat life as precious. Darcy says it is a way of being human like Jesus was, which *included* his mortality (Philippians 2:5-11).

Thomas Merton once said that "too often a legalistic concept of the will of God leads to a hypocritical falsification of the interior life," which tempts us to believe God is a harsh lawgiver or that we are only allowed to sing songs of praise.[10] Merton contended God wants to collaborate with us. Paul describes us as God's servant who works together with him. He uses the word συνεργός (*synergos*), meaning "fellow worker" (Philemon 23-24).[11] We can bring our concerns, questions, and suffering to God. It is one way we become fellow workers with the Divine.

And yet, sometimes God seems most distant in difficulty. A sixteenth century Spanish mystic talked about such moments as dark nights of the soul—John of the Cross saw them as difficult gifts meant to draw us further into connection with God. He said God's apparent absence was not punishment or indifference, but a chance to address disordered loves and ways of coping that keep us separated from God, others, and ourselves.

John didn't minimize the pain of such times. He said of the worst part, "What the sorrowing soul feels most is the conviction that God has rejected it."[12] I read those words for the first time on a flight to Portland during seminary. I turned my body toward the window to mask my sobs. I was desperately wishing someone had shared that wisdom with me before then. It wouldn't have made things easy, but it would have made me less likely to believe God hated me.

John exhorted those who have entered a season of darkness to resist the urge to frantically try returning to past ways of work and worship and to be still. When spiritual darkness presses in and the Spirit seems distant, allow yourself to stop. Don't race to solve your grief or fast-forward to healing. Rest your mind and soul and body.

John of the Cross contended dark nights are worth enduring because new life is on the other side. This is the good fruit that can grow from lament. And it's how we can dare say there is such a thing as redeeming suffering, and even a good death. I'm not encouraging you to take perverse pleasure in pain or become like the dying woman who smiled while seething underneath. But bearing witness to suffering and death, we refuse to make difficult seasons all the more painful by resisting them.

When my friend Jenny's family realized her beloved grandmother's death was near, her granddaughters gathered to be with her. Nana had lived long enough to spend precious years with her great grandchildren. She was ready to say goodbye. They sang her favorite songs, smoothed lotion on her hands, and were simply lovingly present. When they sang "It Is Well," Nana opened her eyes for the first time in hours and took her last breath with the song's closing notes. Her family was with her, accompanying her through a sacred passage.

Of course, some deaths can't be approached this way. Sudden or violent deaths must not be called good. But fear and avoidance of death don't prevent it. And life can be more freely lived by embracing the fulness of the human experience, which includes suffering and the end of life. Which brings us back to Job's story.

After initially bearing silent witness to his pain, Job's friends couldn't suppress their desire for a tidy explanation for his pain. If his trial could be called judgment, they felt safe. So, they harangued him with bad theology. But even in his weakened and grief-stricken state, Job refused to compromise. He kept honoring the tension between God's goodness and the reality of injustice in the world. And he kept telling God his suffering felt unfair.

When Job finally poured out every drop of his grief, his three friends mercifully fell silent after twenty-eight chapters of debate. But a young man named Elihu chose that moment to speak up. He was furious Job called himself righteous. He was mad at the flimsy arguments made by Job's friends. He droned on for seven chapters, explaining Job couldn't be innocent. He said God was always speaking to anyone who would listen. There is some truth in that; God does speak through sacred texts, dreams, the created world, and in countless other ways. But Elihu's god whispered sinister pronouncements, always ready to smite someone, instead of championing widows and orphans.

For Elihu, the realities of Job's sickness and suffering proved he was guilty. He said all who die young perish because of their sin. Too many bereaved parents and grieving spouses have heard similar crushing and absolutely wrong messages. His tirade reminds us that throwing self-righteous judgments and false certainties at those experiencing suffering isn't a new problem.

It isn't that he, or Job's other friends, were completely wrong about God's sovereignty or justice. But in emphasizing power and majesty, they missed God's mercy and kindness. Like Job's other friends, Elihu was terrified to admit pain isn't always divine retribution. That sometimes evil seems to be winning.

The In-Between

Lament is breathing room for grief. It is willing to admit that hope, and a sense of the Spirit's presence, sometimes feel an ocean away. I once heard a teacher say that God has no potential: he meant that God is settled, unchanging, and utterly complete within the Trinity. I believe that's true—and yet God allows himself to be moved by us (Isaiah 43:26; Mark 7:24-30). Our pain, loneliness, and exhaustion all matter to God as much as our joys, dreams, and hopes do.

Like God, we can allow things to shift, developing meaning and clarity over days and months and decades. A process of the dawning of hope, healing, and essential truth-telling has been happening in my soul for years. And I know it is a work that remains unfinished and that will continue. I wonder where you are being invited to allow such things to percolate and deepen with time.

I love that the Psalms take sin and evil seriously. They beg God to deal harshly with the powerful who are manipulating or hurting others. Nancy Lee says such psalms are emotional outlets and convey an appropriate sense of outrage at injustice. She maintains they are also a chance "to turn such desires over to God, who has the power to transform and cleanse the lamenter of destructive feelings and forces."[13]

Sometimes repair and renewal can happen in the briefest of conversations or prayers. But when loss is significant or complex, restoration must happen over months and years, allowing the broken pieces of grief to be formed into a sort of mosaic. The broken pieces that make up mosaics mirror the disorienting fragmentation of grief and the ways that lament can contribute to new life. Terry Tempest Williams calls mosaics "a conversation with time."[14] So are laments. The broken pieces offered as laments honor the past, have courage to live the now authentically, and dare breathe hope for future restoration.

After her husband's sudden death, Jan Richardson wrote, "Grief moves by turns and spirals, a twisting path that I am not sure can even be called a path because it is not always that clear or orderly. Grief is the least linear thing I know."[15] Gena St. David says relationships thrive when we can move between connection, disconnection, and reconnection.[16] That's true of human relationships and it also applies to our connection with God. Lament acknowledges when disconnection or disorientation happen and makes room for reconnection and repair. But grief needs space to birth new life.

Cultivating Healing Together

We can grow our ability to honor our own experiences while also forming more healthy connections with God and others. Healing and renewal will take a unique route within each of us. Therapist Aundi Kolber says the "work of paying compassionate attention is, in a sense, learning to steward for ourselves what God already believes about us—that we're valuable and loved."[17]

It is vulnerable to admit things are broken or wrong or hard. But such confessions make renewal and reconnection possible. Healthy relationships change over time in response to life's circumstances. It happens in human relationships and also with our connection with the Spirit. St. David says that the kind of relationships that foster growth "contribute to our wellness and our maturity and encourage us to be separate individuals *who are also* kind, relational, and collaborate well with others."[18]

Brueggemann and others describe theological perspectives of psalms and other biblical prayers as moving through cycles of orientation—describing the world as it ought to be—and then disorientation and reorientation following injustice or other brokenness. I can't help but notice a common thread between those ideas and St. David's psychological description of relationships as naturally traveling between connection, disconnection, and reconnection. She says we can recognize similar patterns in the natural world, "in the mini-sermon written in the life, death, and rebirth story of butterflies, oak trees, and stars."[19]

The same pattern is also present in the story of Jesus' life, death, and resurrection. The incarnation is God's definitive word on whether the Holy will remain aloof from suffering. Jesus' birth, life, death, and resurrection tell the story of a God who would risk everything to make a way to restore connection and heal brokenness. And it isn't only for those with perfect theology, who never make mistakes, or who are part of the right group. All are welcome to be part of God's family. Jesus told his friends on the night before he died that they would mourn, but that their anguish would turn into joy, like a mom in labor whose pain is eclipsed when she holds her child (John 16:20-22).

Jesus completed the move from orientation and connection by leaving heaven; he faithfully entered disorientation and disconnection through his death; and he returned to reconnection and reorientation in his resurrection and return to heaven. This is the kind of Love that longs to meet us within our griefs, large and small, and carry us to the other side toward newness. In the years I have been learning to lament, I've found it to be a kind of alchemy, slowly transforming love and loss and suffering into hope, renewal, and more love.

Tear Jar Practice

GOD CONSIDERS YOUR TEARS PRECIOUS. Whether you cry often or your tears tend to remain unshed, your grief matters to the Spirit. David declared, "You have kept count of my tossings; put my tears in your bottle. Are they not in your record?" (Psalm 56:8). The Holy One knows every sleepless hour and preserves your tears like treasures.

When you have something complex to grieve, try creating a tear jar. Keep a jar of water and a saltshaker somewhere accessible.

When grief, anxiety, or other painful emotions come, release them as though through tears by shaking a few grains of salt into the water—actual tears are always also welcome. Continue this practice for three days. At the end of the third day, spend a few minutes noticing what it was like to release your grief in this way. You probably won't remember every flash of emotion or thought that accompanied the grains of salt now diluted into the water, but they remain held by Love.

You can pour the salt water out into the sink to represent entrusting your sorrow to the safekeeping of the Divine. If you live near a body of water, you might consider releasing the record of your tears into the flow of the river, lake, or ocean. Remember that unless you have something invasive you want to get rid of, don't pour your saltwater on plant life!

What was this practice like for you? How did you experience the Spirit?

Saltwater Art Practice for Children and Families

Gather paper, brushes, watercolors, water for activating paint and rinsing brushes, and a saltshaker. Invite children to paint for a bit, focusing on something hard that happened or a sad memory.

While they paint, you might invite them to talk about how they expressed their hard feelings about what happened at the time. Did they cry, pound the ground, or run to a quiet place?

Once they are done painting, invite them to sprinkle some grains of salt on the still-wet paint. They might also like to add more water over the salt.

Talk about how tears and other sad and mad feelings are welcome with you, with other safe grownups, and with God. You could read a child-friendly version of Psalm 56:8 (NLT) like "You keep track of all my sorrows. You have collected all my tears in your bottle. You have recorded each one in your book." How is it to think about God caring for their sadness with them?

Return to their painting and notice any ways that the salt has changed the painting. What do they want to remember?

5

Grief Work

There is no past
As long as there are stories. Stories are how we embrace
Each other whether we can touch each other or not; trust
Me on this. I have so often been wrong, but not this time.

BRIAN DOYLE

A WOMAN I HOST in spiritual direction lost her mother suddenly to Covid-19 around eighteen months into the pandemic.[1] The woman and her mom historically had a close relationship but had recent relational distance over their different views about precautions against the virus.

When the woman's mom got sick, she deteriorated quickly and died before her daughter could see her again. This adult daughter felt an overwhelming need for closure. She knew she needed spiritual practices to help her grieve her mother's loss. She explained her mom had often taken her horseback riding as a child, and talked about how she'd decided to go for a ride recently on her mom's birthday and sensed a peaceful presence and bittersweet grief as she rode while the wind caressed her face. She was following a trustworthy impulse toward an embodied experience of grief and gratitude.

Loss is tender and sacred, whether it is of a beloved friend or family member or a cherished dream or relationship. It deserves to be brought into the light and fully experienced over time. Our modern tendency to smile and power through is more harmful than we often realize.

As she was coming to terms with a series of griefs including her own chronic illness, church planter Aubrey Sampson described manically trying to suppress her grief and uncertainty through a combination of upbeat show tunes and cringy sayings like "every cloud has a silver lining." She was working hard to "prove how okay and optimistic I am. To keep the spotlight on the Good while ignoring the Bad."[2] Her wake-up call to enter a season of healing lament came when her husband starkly told her that her refusal to accept reality was hurting her and those around her.

The reality is that lament can paradoxically help us be happier over time. Psychologists have found that happiness is not merely the absence of negative emotions but can also be "feeling unpleasant emotions when they are appropriate."[3] A crosscultural study unsurprisingly indicated a clear preference for pleasant emotions. But it also found that people were happier when their emotions were in keeping with their circumstances. In other words, they reported more happiness when they felt what seemed appropriate for their context and situation *even if* those emotions were anger or sadness.[4] Feeling our feelings as they truly are isn't only more honest, it's one way to more everyday peace.

Rejecting Indifference

I started feeling invited to process grief in a fresh way a few years ago when the world seemed constantly on fire. Maybe there wasn't more suffering than before, but there was a sense of a steadily increasing volume. Bad news felt more pervasive.

As she reflected on the decades since the 9/11 attacks, Sasha Sagan wrote, "Every week, a headline seems to briefly shake the earth, before being overshadowed and falling away down the memory hole."[5] She said since we are constantly bombarded by news of shootings, wars, oppression, and other atrocities, most of us survive by being in a state of perpetual forgetting.

I often wince internally when I get a news alert, bracing for bad news. But with exceptions for necessary breaks, I don't often turn off the notifications. I don't believe it is helpful or wise to systematically opt out of knowing about suffering in the world. My teachers of color have helped me realize that the possibility of tuning out is more available to me as a privileged person. That "good vibes only" works if your life is relatively free from suffering and oppression.

In that vein, Austin Channing Brown describes a high school trip exploring Black history in the south. After an exhibit on lynching, she was surprised and heartbroken to hear white students deflecting blame from themselves. She mourned that they "reached for anything that would distance themselves from the pain and anger of the moment; anything to ward off the guilt and shame, the shock and devastation."[6]

In the Psalms, David lamented those who chose indifference to pain and suffering. I don't want to be detached from what those who suffer are experiencing. I feel responsible to stay reasonably informed. And it's simultaneously important to recognize that this choice has an impact on the soul, and calibrate rest and care accordingly.

Nadia Bolz-Weber says, "I don't think the human psyche was developed to be able to hold all the information that's available to us right now—in terms of every form of injustice and violence and human suffering that happens all across the planet."[7] She argues we're meant to handle the ebbs and flows of life in a single neighborhood or village, trusting that not everything is ours to care about and considering what is ours to do rather than being over-responsible.

In Acts, when Agabus accurately prophesied a coming famine to the church in Antioch, their response was to focus on how they could help those who would be impacted by it and to send relief for those in the most need (Acts 11:28-29). N. T. Wright points out that "They do *not* say either 'This must be a sign that the Lord is coming back soon!' or 'This must mean that we have sinned and need to repent'—or even 'this will give us a great opportunity to tell the wider world that everyone has sinned and needs to repent.'"[8] They didn't spiral on why something bad was happening, but on how they could help, trusting that one crucial way God would be working was through them.

And yet in between learning of another's suffering and acting for solace or justice (or praying for those who can act), there is the need to pause, to breathe in grace for whatever arises in us in response and to breathe out whatever needs to move through us or be laid down. Sometimes that needs to become a longer prayer. But often, a simple, wordless petition is enough.

Practicing Vulnerability

Lament can be simply speaking grief like Job's cry that began with the haunting words cursing his birth. When David learned his son Absalom had been killed in the attempt to usurp David's own throne, he cried out in anguish. "The king covered his face, and the king cried with a loud voice, 'O my son Absalom, O Absalom, my son, my son!'" (2 Samuel 19:4).

My seminary cohort was encouraged to prepare ourselves for an emotionally intense course near the end of our program. The reading list included texts on the Holocaust, marital affairs, and the dangers and abuses of cheap grace. The instructor told us during our first meeting that we would be asked to share a personal story with our classmates halfway through the term. We would be invited to tell of a time when we were angry or disappointed with God and when we first sensed God's loving presence afterward. It was by no means a small request.

But it was a good requirement for those of us being trained to be pastors, chaplains, and spiritual directors, to practice authentically sharing our own hard stories. It would help us remember how taxing that kind of vulnerability can be. And as spiritual leaders, we needed to appreciate the extent to which suffering, loss, and even disappointment or anger with God are part of life after the Garden. As Fleming Rutledge contends, "One of the reasons the Christian gospel makes sense is that it takes fully into account the sadness and brokenness and downright wickedness of this life."[9]

Most of us had been learning together for years. Many were trusted colleagues and friends. Yet it was still incredibly heavy. Over the course of many hours, we bore witness to stories of catastrophic accidents, destructive choices, miscarriages, assaults, and precious dreams lost. We also heard stories of friendship, grace, and holy consolation. The sense of the Holy was palpable. There was a moment when one student was clearly struggling to begin sharing her story. She is a wonderfully plainspoken and dependable pastor and a good leader. She sat between me and another pastor. As she took in shuddering breaths, the two of us began to deepen our breaths as we silently prayed on either side of her, asking God to send her comfort. Soon the three of us were breathing in unison, each breath a silent prayer for grace and courage.

Out of that sacred space, she told of heartbreak and loss few would have imagined to be part of her story. Hers was, in Leonard Cohen's well-known phrase, a "broken hallelujah," with no clear resolution but rather an invitation to live with loss and find other joys and affirmations of life in the midst of them. She later told us that our wordless prayers had infused her with the courage to speak and a sense of being held by trusted others as she told her story.

We need to speak and sing and otherwise respond to our losses. Not because any of us desire to ruminate on sadness, but because this is the good work of metabolizing pain so that it can be, over time and with the help of the Spirit, transformed into goodness and grace.[10] My friend and fellow spiritual director Lacy Finn Borgo is fond of paraphrasing Trevor Hudson's wisdom that we don't learn from our experiences, we learn from experiences that we have *reflected* on. Lament is a way to give suffering and losses their due attention.

Later that week in our seminary classroom, we were invited to consider the ways that reconciliation is needed among women and men, particularly in the church. Those who had told us to prepare for having our emotions stirred sure hadn't exaggerated. Our instructor invited us to spend time journaling about where we saw the need for healing among genders, what gets in the way of it, and where each of us felt most challenged. Then she introduced us to the art of writing pantoums. A *pantoum* is an accessible poetic form that takes lines from something like a journaling exercise and organizes them in a repeated order.

They originated from the fifteenth century Malaysian *pantun* that were "adapted by French poets [e.g., Victor Hugo and Charles Baudelaire] and occasionally imitated in English."[11] The poet Edward Hirsch says, "The pantoum is always looking back over its shoulder, and thus it is well-suited to evoke a sense of times past. It is always turning back while moving forward; that's why it works so well for poignant poems of loss . . . [and] departure."[12]

We were asked to create a pantoum using six phrases from our writing on gender. When I pulled out my class notes, I was struck by phrases like "oppressed and ignored," "proclaiming openness but practicing patriarchy," and "women are [painted as] temptresses." Perhaps most stunning in retrospect was the line "I limit myself." I was beginning to recognize the extent to which I had internalized messages which demeaned me and urged me to suppress my gifts. I wonder where you have received destructive messages that continue to swirl within you? What harmful beliefs is God inviting you to unlearn so that you can be freer to express the good gifts within you? Lament can be a beginning of healing renewal in such places.

We turned in our pantoums anonymously. Our professor read every single one out loud. It was powerful. I remember one kindhearted pastor weeping aloud at the idea that his wife had almost certainly internalized some of the destructive perspectives he heard being described by his female fellow students. It was a recognition that stirred him to seek ways to help her and the other women in his congregation find more freedom. It makes my heart happy to know that his gentle soul is now leading a church in the Midwest.

We closed our time with a handwashing ritual, a collective reminder of our baptism. I love the way such everyday actions can become imbued with the Holy. The best rituals are often the simplest. A cleansing dip in the water can symbolize salvation, a sip of wine and bite of bread surfacing the mystical substance of eternal life. I am convinced that a return and reimagination of rituals is sorely needed in our digital age. We need to become reacquainted with our physical bodies apart from our devices and technologies and remember they are worthy of love and care. We need to be free to create new rhythms that connect us to what is sacred within and without.

Lament and Hope

As essential as hope is, it is not the starting point for healing. It can't be. But there is a better way that begins with lament. The night is often lonely; it's frightening at times. But darkness doesn't have the last word. One of the things that makes lament surprisingly life-giving is the invitation to hold hope and lament in tension without rejecting either. This requires cultivating hospitality within our souls to experience both in due season.

They often happen sequentially. And sometimes lament and hope can even coexist.

The one who would become Jesus' mother acknowledged future goodness and grace alongside mystery and suffering. When an angel showed up telling Mary that she was favored, Mary was anything but a passive recipient of that proclamation. She was perplexed (διαταράσσω [*diatarassō*]), and pondered (διαλογίζομαι [*dialogizomai*]) the strange greeting (Luke 1:29). It wasn't some mild confusion. She was "acutely distressed" and "deeply troubled."[13] And she didn't ignore her emotions even as she kept listening. After hearing that God's favor meant she was to carry a child who would be God's son, and that her formerly barren relative Elizabeth was expecting a child, she responded with resolve (Luke 1:38).

Mary's next move was to pack a bag and rush to her relative's house in the hill country. She had the journey to continue contemplating everything. She wanted to see Elizabeth's miraculously swelling belly with her own eyes. And she also wanted to spend time with someone who understood, more than others possibly could, what was happening and could help her make sense of it all.

When she arrived in Judea, everything was as the angel had told her it would be. Her heart full, Mary poured out a song of praise for the kind of God who would lift the lowly, scatter the proud, and fill the hungry with good things (Luke 1:46-55). She stayed three more months, maybe waiting until she could help deliver Elizabeth's child who would become known as the Baptizer. They had plenty of time to ponder together what God was up to in and through them.

Carrying a child is waiting and it is also hard work. Grief and lament are also frequently slow and quiet labor. They require patience and strength. Mary's cultivation of her capacity for that kind of patient pondering didn't stop after Jesus' birth.

When she delivered the promised child, they were in the hometown of Israel's beloved king, David, a place associated with royalty. But Jesus' makeshift cradle was a feeding trough. When his birth was first announced not to monarchs but to poor shepherds sleeping outside with their flocks, angels confirmed Mary's conviction that God's goodness through her son would prioritize holy reversals. The angels told them the Messiah was born *to them*. Unlike the hesitancy of religious leaders or the grasp for control of political leaders, the shepherds trusted— and found the child just as he'd been described. They immediately told Mary and Joseph, and anyone else who would listen, about the angels' message.

And Mary treasured and pondered their words. She still had more questions than answers. But that didn't stop her from appreciating all she'd heard and seen. She was preserving her memories and keeping them safe inside her soul.[14] Mary was memorizing all that had happened. It was clear she'd need to know these things in the future, allowing understanding to deepen over time.

She was beginning to see the extent to which she was part of something wonderful, realizing that though the plan she'd been invited into was occasionally confusing and often difficult, it was poised to end in goodness and mercy. We are also invited to fan the flames of hope even when grief is longer and more complicated than we wish it were.

As she did at the angel's greeting, Mary also carefully considered the shepherd's message, holding together a joyful, hope-filled posture with one that was willing to enter mystery and lament. She was considering the implications of Jesus' birth, reflecting on it all "seriously [and] deeply."[15] She'd need to hold her anguish at the slaughter of innocent children in Bethlehem alongside her relief that Jesus survived. She would need to recollect the wonder of shepherd's prophecies and the gifts and worship of strangers alongside the quiet joys of holding her beloved firstborn child.

She needed to carry the awe of angelic visions alongside her confusion when Jesus didn't turn out to be the kind of Messiah she expected. There is freedom in that kind of paradox. It honors the reality of suffering, giving pain the loving attention it requires. It also refuses to ignore the beauty of life that endures and hope that is not quenched. It is a way to avoid the danger of the temptations to despair at one extreme and of clinging to toxic positivity on the other.

Patient Courage

The same Greek word for Mary's treasuring appears in Jesus' story about the wineskins. It seems he learned from his mom's habits of thoughtful contemplation and holding complex ideas together. He said new wine belongs in new wineskins so that both the container and the wine are preserved and protected (Matthew 9:16-17).

No one wants new wine. It tastes terrible. It's the kind of vinegary concoction that Jesus rejected on the cross. New wine is put into new wineskins so that both can ripen and mature.

Jesus was saying new life could be formed, but it would take time. Lament is like that. It can't be rushed without doing violence to the soul.

Hope and lament can be developed together. And like all the art and science and history of winemaking, lament isn't a one-size-fits all equation. It takes patience and willingness to enter a work that bears fruit worth waiting for.

A friend sent me a postcard from Dresden on the fourth anniversary of our fire. She wrote of how the German city was being restored to its former beauty stone by stone. She said it reminded her of my story—one of rebuilding slowly, using old and new bricks. It's like Jesus taught, "Therefore every scribe who has become a disciple in the kingdom of heaven is like the master of a household who brings out of his treasure what is new and what is old" (Matthew 13:52).

When disaster happens, returning to the past isn't possible. But finding a new normal is. You can rebuild brick by brick, preserving what can be preserved and using new material where it's needed. You can carry forward the best parts of what or who was lost while also growing and changing where necessary.

Hope, lament, and even joy can be held together. But when they are, one voice is usually speaking louder than the other. As Mary and Jesus demonstrate, maintaining them requires holding them in tension, refusing to silence pain or ignore goodness and beauty.

The good work of lament is embracing audacious hope *eventually* and *over time*. An invitation to trust is never shouted. Faith and hope can't be forced. Eugene Peterson describes hope not as a dream or fantasy but "imagination put in the harness of faith."[16] It is a willingness to let God work in God's time and God's way. Any encouragement to trust or joy must come on the other side of weeping with those who weep. It takes courageous patience to let life be the hard, beautiful, complicated thing it is.

Pantoum Practice

To write a pantoum, journal about your grief as you did in the psalm practice at the end of chapter three. A pantoum is like a haiku with a less structured form. Review your journaling and choose six phrases that stand out to you—they don't need to be complete sentences. You can arrange your phrases using the following model (or choose your own order):

Stanza 1

line 1 (new line):______________________________
line 2 (new line):______________________________
line 3 (new line):______________________________
line 4 (new line):______________________________

Stanza 2

line 5 (repeat line 2, stanza 1):____________________
line 6 (new line):______________________________
line 7 (repeat line 4, stanza 1):____________________
line 8 (new line):______________________________

Stanza 3

line 9 (repeat line 6, stanza 2):____________________
line 10 (repeat line 3, stanza 1):___________________

line 11 (repeat line 8, stanza 2):______________________
line 12 (repeat line 1, stanza 1):______________________

Try reading your pantoum aloud to yourself even if it feels a little awkward. There is power in hearing your own voice articulate your grief. You can also find someone trustworthy to share it with.

Clapping Practice for Families and Children

Invite children to ask their *why*, *how long*, or *when* questions, then to tell what feels scary or uncertain that they hope won't happen. Then they can name a reassuring thought—something they know. Finally ask what they hope or wish. You can write these down or simply listen with care.

You might also invite any grownups present, including you, to ask a question and name a worry, a comforting truth, and a hope. Choose three or four of these and chant them out loud together while clapping hands, slapping your legs, or clapping hands with each other. It could go something like this:

Line 1 (a *why*, *how long*, or *when* question): chant it together while clapping hands

Line 2 (something they hope won't happen): chant it together while patting legs

Line 3 (a reassuring thought): chant it together while clapping hands with a partner

Line 4 (a hope): chant it together while clapping hands

6

Trauma and the Courage to Lament

It's hard to keep the eyes clear
when they live
so close to the brain
where circuits spark with information
piled up for processing
and thought-lines clog with questions
that play hockey between one's ears
in the dark hours.

JAN RICHARDSON

WHEN I WAS TRYING to make sense of all my family had been through, I set up countless meetings with friends, mentors, even distant acquaintances—anyone who would talk to me. I was desperate for help and relief, something to illuminate the way ahead.

I was grasping at straws. As it was for Job, my unraveling made me an outcast. I think my desperation made me a little ridiculous. I could tell some wondered if my suffering might be contagious. Others radiated judgment that we'd left the church we helped plant, without asking if there might have been a good reason. In those moments, I understood Job's impulse to plead for help and solidarity all too well (Job 19:19-21).

What I needed to know, as I frantically tried to understand our suffering and how to fix it, is that it was okay to stop. I asked my spiritual director at the time for practices I should engage. Without missing a beat, he told me I should take more walks outside and more naps. I thought he was joking. When it was clear he wasn't, I was unconvinced. Wouldn't that be lazy and frivolous? But I tried it. And started realizing how bone-crushingly weary I was. I started letting myself be a human being instead of eternally doing.

The action my grief required was stillness. I needed to rest and heal. It allowed breathing room for more perspective. I needed to stop holding together the shattered pieces of my life and let the shards fall to the ground. Only then would it be possible to start picking up the pieces. God was often silent in those days. And yet, I can now see that the Spirit was also *in* the silence.

I wonder if you need permission to let something be broken or unsolved for a time, to stop striving. Many of us are not okay right now.

And it's vital to talk with the young ones in our lives about the good and the hard, too. Silence doesn't protect them. Psychologist Lisa Miller says if "a child doesn't hear a parent discussing a topic, then the child assumes that topic is not important."[1] We need to be engaging grief faithfully, finding ways to express painful emotions together.

Beauty can and does follow ashes, but only on the other side of naming and living through the fullness of devastation. As is always true with sorrow, the only way forward is through. Lament can be healing in cases of anxiety, trauma, abuse, and other types of psychological distress. Since I'm writing as a spiritual director and teacher rather than a therapist or psychologist, I am a fellow learner with you in these things.

Mind, Body, and Spirit

Our minds, bodies, and spirits are wonderfully interconnected. Neuroscience sheds light on how painful events get processed, leading to more mental, physical, and spiritual health. It starts with recognizing that our brains have three distinct yet unified parts, like the Trinity. Maybe that's another glimpse of ways we are made in God's image.

The brain stem develops first and is directly connected to input from the rest of the body, controlling things like breathing, digestion, and heartbeats. The limbic (emotional) system develops second: it is focused on forming mutual connections of nurture and love, beginning with primary caregivers. And the neocortex organizes speech, "writing, planning, and reasoning [as well as] awareness [and] . . . what we know as will."[2] This third part of the brain develops last and continues maturing into early adulthood.

Stress impacts brains and bodies. And that's not always a bad thing. Remember the story of Goldilocks looking for the just right amount of everything in the three bears' home? There is a "Goldilocks range" in which we're not stagnant or overwhelmed. With too little stress, we get bored and growth languishes. But when there's too much stress, parts of our brains related to survival get overactivated. When that happens, Gena St. David says that neural links "related to relationality, kindness, creativity, and access to joy" flounder.[3]

That means that if anyone is consistently under- or overwhelmed, learning and growth become difficult or even temporarily impossible. St. David says nerves that activate together more often are like highways that become smoother and easier to travel over time, while those that fire together less frequently are more like unpaved roads or overgrown pathways. But highways can be dismantled, and dusty paths paved. This is the hope of redemption.

Most animals respond to too much stress by calling for help. If an infant dog, cat, or human is separated from parents, they signal their distress by crying.[4] When they get older, they'll learn to stay safe by either defending against the threat, running away, or seeking peace. Their bodies learn to enter fight, flight, or fawn postures—or at the opposite extreme, freeze—when faced with danger.

When that happens to a person, the reasoning brain stops calling the shots. That means we've lost connection with the parts of us that help us problem solve and gotten "stuck ruminating on our problems instead."[5]

In a hyperaroused, too-much state of fight, flight, or fawn, the brain stem, which operates underneath and beyond the control of the logical mind, "takes over, mobilizing muscles, heart, and lungs . . ." to act in self-defense.[6] That can feel like an adrenaline rush, racing heart, trembling, a strong urge to move, anger, anxiety or fear, or an overwhelming need to appease people and avoid conflict.

If we don't get the help we need, eventually we freeze. That's when the body moves into survival mode because of extreme physical or psychological danger. The nervous system reaches beneath the lungs and diaphragm to the stomach and other digestive organs and "drastically reduces metabolism throughout the body," telling the body to prepare for a famine of food and drink or love and safety.[7] This can look like sluggishness, depression, exhaustion, mental fog, a sense of watching the self from a distance or of feeling frozen in one spot.[8]

Again, these responses aren't necessarily bad. In a crisis, they can be lifesaving. But when we get stuck reliving difficult moments or become hypervigilant following difficult events, it can be dangerous for us and others. Resmaa Menakem says that traumatized people keep experiencing past pain as if it were still happening in the present.[9]

Cultivating Safety

A grieving, anxious, or traumatized person is often flooded with stress responses that make peace, calm, and joy impossible for the moment. Traumatized people retain stress hormones longer than those who haven't experienced that kind of suffering.[10] They are left in an ongoing state of alert that isn't safe physically or spiritually. This shows up differently for different people. For some, it manifests as unexplained anger or feeling physically overheated. For others, it will show up as isolating socially or avoiding conflict. And for some, it will look like numbing, or being emotionally shut down.

But none of this is a life sentence. The good news is that the brain is wonderfully resilient. The distress of unhelpful connections in our brains can be undone and new patterns formed. More capacity for addressing our griefs and losses can be cultivated. It starts with that Goldilocks range of stress that's sometimes called a "window of tolerance"—each of us has one. In pain or stress, we have less capacity and naturally get overwhelmed faster. The solution is not to push harder, which only prolongs difficulty. Rather, it is to give your body and soul breathing room. Consider this your invitation to rest, show yourself compassion, and not always be producing.

Aundi Kolber says when you're in your window of tolerance, you'll feel things like competence, strength, curiosity, a sense of relaxation, balance, hopefulness, and readiness for appropriate risks.[11] There are lots of ways to gently and gradually expand your Goldilocks zone. Some engage the logical mind, some the emotional mind, and others the physical body. You can experiment with some of the possibilities that follow to find what works well for you.

Finding more capacity for navigating stress requires starting with more safety for the physical body. This is especially important when losses are complex and layered. Many therapists have found telling stories of pain are essential but often not enough. And moving too quickly in talking about painful events can actually make things worse. As important as storytelling is, it alone can't "alter the automatic physical and hormonal responses of bodies that remain hypervigilant, prepared to be assaulted or violated at any time."[12] Healing requires allowing the physical body to learn that danger has passed. Patient pacing is key.

Kolber suggests something called containment when you feel overwhelmed: picturing something strong enough to hold your painful experiences, such as a treasure chest, safe, or God's hands.[13] Once you've selected a container, imagine putting grief inside it. If the container doesn't feel strong enough, add another layer of protection—you could make your container be on the moon or at the bottom of the ocean. The next time you're feeling anxious, imagine putting your hard emotions into your container until you can relax, knowing you can return to the memory later when you're ready. A breath prayer, like those at the end of chapter one, can be helpful after containment exercises.

Mindfulness and meditation can also be helpful by cultivating gentle, nonjudgmental attention to the present. Studies have shown that "meditation causes significant reduction in symptoms of anxiety and panic" for many.[14] Centering prayer is one way to practice mindfulness, by focusing on a prayer word or phrase such as a favorite name for God.

Yoga and other moving meditations can help you return to the present moment and a sense of being alive that can serve to calm anxiety. I started practicing yoga years ago; it has been life changing. As an abuse survivor, I wasn't comfortable in my own skin. I was physically clumsy, a common aftereffect of trauma. Yoga helped me relearn how to listen to my body, attend to my breath, and notice how different emotions could be connected with physical postures. It taught me I could develop more resilience. Van der Kolk regularly prescribes a yoga practice for his patients.[15] He notes that trauma can make people feel like they're stuck replaying their worst moments, but that in "yoga you learn that sensations rise to a peak and then fall."[16]

Another way to expand your window of tolerance is talking about pain with others. This makes a way for fresh clarity to emerge. Through losing both parents at a young age and in her work as a therapist, Claire Bidwell Smith has found that anxiety is often associated with the death of loved ones, since it puts us in the vulnerable place of facing mortality.[17] Over the years, much of her work has been around creating compassionate room for people to tell about their last moments with loved ones. I have also noticed, in my work as a spiritual director, the need for stories of suffering and loss to be empathetically heard.

When you're ready to process a painful part of your story, Smith suggests asking what the beginning of the story is.[18] Are there aspects of the story you tend to leave out? Consider whether there are parts that aren't true anymore or that you see differently now. Ask yourself if rather than focusing on pain and loss, you could expand your focus to the *life* of the loved one or the loss's larger context. Have there been gifts within suffering or that have emerged over time? If your story involved abuse, go slowly, paying special attention to your Goldilocks range of not too little or too much stress.

You could start by journaling your experience. Then find a trustworthy person to share your story with. That kind of human connection sparks emotional regulation in which a second person's compassionate presence positively impacts hormones, heart function, sleep, and immunity.[19] Relationships matter at a cellular level. If your story is complicated or especially painful, consider also sharing it with a therapist, pastor, or spiritual director. And throughout, try inviting the Spirit into all this sacred storytelling.

Go Gently

Caution and care are necessary when lamenting trauma, abuse, or other vulnerable things. Van der Kolk says, "It takes enormous trust and courage to allow yourself to remember."[20] Pay attention to embodied and emotional safety as you explore loss and brokenness. If you find yourself leaving a calm, here-and-now state of attention when remembering a story, stop and engage your senses. You might find it helpful to stretch, take a walk, or make a cup of tea. Once you feel more settled, you can return to what you were thinking, praying, and feeling your way through. A friend who was diagnosed with PTSD following military service says it's crucial *not* to dig for repressed memories. This is another way that lament invites us to patience. If events are inaccessible or there are parts of your past that are hazy or missing, prayerfully invite them to unfurl themselves over time. And never stay in those places alone. Share what you're discovering with trustworthy others.

I now know ways to quell a panic attack when I'm having one. It starts with accepting what's happening and remembering nothing is physically wrong, once it's confirmed that is the case. It's important to breathe deeply, finding something that connects you to your physical space. Smith suggests eating some chocolate, taking a bath or shower, or playing with your pet. Let someone know you're having a hard time. It's helpful to change your environment—getting outside, putting bare feet on grass, or lying down with a cozy blanket. You can also try picturing something calming and remembering that panic attacks don't last forever.

As you surface tender parts of your history, proceed gently. Fleeting feelings of hopelessness or depression are to be expected. But if you are having suicidal thoughts, please reach out for professional help. Warning signs of serious depression to watch for include sleeplessness or sleeping too much, alcohol or drug abuse, loss of appetite, social withdrawal, and intense sensations of hopelessness.[21] If that's you or someone you love, reach out to a therapist or grief counselor right away. In the United States, you can dial 988 or go online to https://988lifeline.org.

In all these things, listen to your body and let your soul speak. They can tell you whether you're feeling safe or not. Fears and stuck thoughts need breathing room. This is the good and necessary work of healing. It is not weakness but the best kind of strength.

When he took on a human body, Jesus decided not to exploit his divinity (Philippians 2:5-11). He chose solidarity with our humanity including our physicality and revealed what it means to be human when he did. For us, the way forward is not ignoring our bodies or emotional pain. The Holy One wants to meet us in those places and stay with us as hope and renewal return.

Terra Divina Practice

THIS SPIRITUAL PRACTICE will help you slow down and savor the beauty of the natural world. The Japanese practice of forest bathing is more than a walk, it's a way of paying attention to surroundings and senses.[1] There's something trustworthy about connecting with the Holy outdoors since the human story began in a garden. Cole Arthur Riley says, "I like to think of God hunched over in the garden, fingernails hugging the brown soil, mighty hands cradling mud like it's the last flame in a windstorm."[2]

You might be familiar with the practice of lectio divina. It's a contemplative way of engaging a Bible passage or another sacred reading with four movements. The first is reading the passage aloud (*lectio*), listening for a word or phrase that stands out. Next is reflecting (*meditatio*), when the passage is read again while considering how the words speak to your life as it is today. Third is responding (*oratio*), when the passage is read with attention to how you want to respond to what you've heard. The passage is read a final time as you rest (*contemplatio*) in its goodness, thanking God for what you have received. Visio divina follows the same four movements using art or another image.

Terra divina uses these four movements to engage nature as another way God speaks. (You might be thinking I just made up a spiritual practice and named it after myself, but it didn't originate with me.) *Terra* means "earth" in Latin and can refer to dirt, clay, or the planet as a whole. But if you want to imagine that I'm figurately joining you and cheering you on, feel free!

Find a time when you have at least fifteen minutes available. You don't need any special supplies, but you may want a journal, writing utensils, or paint or markers. You can bring a picnic blanket or camp chair if you'd like; allow this be playful and lighthearted.

Begin with a leisurely walk. Put away your devices and headphones for now. Enjoy the landscape and let your senses be engaged. When you feel ready, let your eye be drawn to something. It could be flower, a branch covered with buds, a feather, or a patch of grass. Since you're going to want to spend several minutes with this object, choose something that won't hop or fly away. Find a place to settle comfortably to contemplate the object.

First, notice its texture, colors, size, and so on. Let your attention focus on the object as a whole. Take several moments to reflect. What do you notice?

Next, consider what God wants to say through this object for your life today. Let your gaze be drawn to its various details, allowing yourself to be curious and to wonder. Don't be in a hurry.

Now reflect on how you want to respond to what you've sensed from the Spirit. What do you want to tell God? How do you want to be changed or carry this moment with you?

Finally, allow your gaze to take in the object for a few final breaths, simply resting in its beauty and God's presence with you.

You might journal what you've noticed. You could also draw a simple sketch of your object to take with you. And if you can't get outside for some reason, you can engage terra divina inside with a plant, a piece of fruit, or even a beloved pet.

Terra Divina Practice for Children and Families

Terra divina is a wonderful activity to engage with children. Let them lead the way with wonder!

Take a walk exploring your neighborhood or a park or even a familiar room together. Notice how warm or cool it is, the light, and the colors and textures around you. You don't need any supplies other than time and attention, but you may want to bring a picnic blanket to sit on and some paper and crayons or colored pencils.

Invite the children to be watching for something that captures their attention. It could be something they've never noticed before or it could be a favorite tree or hillside. Remember that since you'll be spending a few minutes with it, try to choose something that can't hop or fly away!

Once they've picked an object to spend a few minutes enjoying, invite them to settle in and really notice it. What colors do they see in it? If it's safe to touch, is it rough or smooth or something else? What does it smell like? What else do they notice about it?

Then, invite the child to wonder about the goodness their object brings to the world. Remember together that God made the world with love and called all creation *good*. What is God wanting to say to them through their object today?

Now, invite them to think about what they want to say back to God. What do they want to remember? They can talk with God whenever they want to—God always listens with love.

Last, encourage them to spend a few final moments with their object, enjoying its goodness.

If you've brought supplies, they could draw a picture of their object. If not, invite them to take a picture of it with their minds so that they can return to it anytime they want to.

7

Lamenting When Community Is Toxic

Quick, God, I need your helping hand!
The last decent person just went down,
All the friends I depended on gone.

PSALM 12:1 MSG

THE CHURCH HAS BEEN a place of hope and connection for me since I was a kid. There is goodness in a community gathered to love God, care for each other, and make earth a little more like heaven. I've been part of churches with bowling alleys and skating rinks, ones focused on studying the Bible, and ones that emphasized service on behalf of others. I've been part of meetings that gathered in schools, theaters, and community centers as well as those that met in more traditional church buildings. I've worshiped with those I have a lot in common with and those who are nothing like me. I've served and led. I've given a lot of my life and received so much grace and goodness in return.

When a job change took us to a new city many years ago, my family connected with a church that was just getting started.

My husband was soon asked to become an elder and I started serving. Our daughter helped create the youth group. We poured our lives into building the community. We taught. My husband preached. I created curricula and articulated vision. I ran the website and wrote most of its content. For years, I led a wonderful team of coders who maintained it.

We were working to create a safe and inviting space for worship and connection with God and others. We taught people how to study the Bible for themselves. We explored women in leadership, and advocated for emotional health, more inclusivity in leadership, and a high value for God's holiness. We felt incredibly honored to help shepherd our community. It seemed like exactly what we'd always been meant to do.

But somewhere along the way, values of empowered humility, radical holiness, and expansive love started getting more muted. People who didn't fit the increasingly rigid mold started getting sidelined. People were burned out, used up, and then discarded.

Many of us ached for a return to the humility, grace, and sense of being a part of something good that God was doing that had characterized our culture in earlier stages. We voiced concerns about harmful patterns. And while many of our misgivings were validated, not much meaningful change happened. We looked very successful and were growing quickly, and there was undeniably good fruit to point toward. But all was not well.

Jesus and Mars Hill

Last year, I spent a lot of cool fall evenings walking the trails near my home while listening to a podcast series, *The Rise and*

Fall of Mars Hill, bear witness to stories of spiritual growth and hopeful beginnings tainted by spiritual abuse.[1] When I pressed play for the first episode, I was dropped back into my years of blood, sweat, and tears poured into church formation in a leadership community that ended up having more in common with the Seattle megachurch called Mars Hill than I wished it had.

I had participated in a few key events connected to Mars Hill, and I had been troubled by the way their pastor Mark Driscoll went beyond simply disassociating with former ministry colleagues because of theological differences, to mocking and belittling them. I'd also read some of the work Driscoll disparaged and knew he was misrepresenting parts of them. His now well-known rage was palpably below the surface, and it was clear to me that he was dangerous. My concerns grew as I heard more of his teaching, especially since my church was considering joining his church-planting network.

To my sorrow, our community did join Driscoll's network. When listening to the podcast about his ministry, I learned to skip its introduction featuring Mark's screaming rants at his congregation. They were too close to home—I was all too familiar with character issues being minimized because a ministry seemed fruitful and pastors whose bad behavior was dismissively excused as anger problems. I had also heard of rage framed as someone being "prophetic." Behaviors like these were often justified when someone was a gifted preacher or leader.

I could relate to the manipulation and increasing emphases on numbers and production, green rooms and security, of a pressurized environment where volunteers like me were used and abused. Like Mars Hill, my church also began with a commitment to staying small and local, but ended up becoming a multisite megachurch.

Chuck DeGroat, a therapist specializing in healing spiritual abuse, says *narcissism* can be enabled and even elevated in worship communities with a narcissist being framed as "charismatic, gifted, confident, smart, strategic, agile, and compelling."[2] When someone like that is presented as a spiritual leader, their bad behavior is often tolerated, excused, or covered up by others. That was the case at Mars Hill and it had happened at my church and many others, too. DeGroat says narcissists are often inconsistent and impulsive. They praise and then withdraw. They feel justified intimidating anyone they see as inferior. They also frequently exhibit "fauxnerability," a manipulative version of vulnerability intended to control others by garnering their sympathy.[3]

When I think about narcissism in the church a number of faces come to mind, but I remember one man in particular who is one of the most manipulative people I have ever met. I would find myself agreeing with this pastor in person. But it was as if a sort of spell was lifted after I left his presence. I shared that sense with a few trusted others and discovered I was not alone. They'd had similar experiences of feeling pressured to agree with him and of his uncanny ability to persuade. His sway was magnified as he hired friends, family members, and men he'd mentored.

People like that pastor are confusing. It's hard to wrap our minds around "a smart, seemingly wise and influential person . . . who was at the same time manipulative, abusive, and conniving."[4] Charm and rage don't seem like they can coexist, but they can for narcissists and there was more than one serving in leadership at my church. When leaders operate in toxic ways, they often attract others with similar tendencies.

More Than a Few Bad Apples

As more staff were added to support our expanding congregation, I started being marginalized as a troublemaker. I remember regularly meeting with another elder's wife around that time. We begged God to heal our community. But our prayers weren't getting answered as we hoped. And I was starting to wonder if I was participating in harmful patterns by staying.

In those days, my thoughts returned to a tense meeting years before in which a volunteer voiced her concerns about several pastors. At the time, I urged her to forgive them, give them room to grow, and to trust their spiritual authority. I was surprised by her furious reaction, but she had discerned dangerous patterns before I realized how damaging they were.

It was a church that wouldn't fully empower my leadership or that of other women because of our gender. And it was made up of mostly white middle- or upper-class people; it was a place where a leader could make a racist joke and frame it as innocent since he had close friends of other ethnicities.

Like Mars Hill, there was a "pile of dead bodies" outside the back door of our church who had been encouraged to be workaholics for Jesus. I heard the phrase repeatedly back then, not realizing it was a paraphrase of Mark's own infamous words. As it was at Mars Hill, there had been an open secret in our church of people being driven to perform and pressed not to take time off.

I understood all too well how members of the community and staff could experience genuinely life-giving worship and connection, unaware of power plays and toxic behavior happening behind the scenes. And I knew how leaders could become disillusioned, jaded, and then horrified at awakening to the harm they'd been part of creating and to the extent of their own woundedness.

At one point, an elder family who had been faithful and gracious leaders for years resigned in exhaustion. Because neither had attended seminary and one of their vocations was considered less prestigious, their leadership had become sidelined. When Kyle later stepped down from the elder board, that man stopped everything and drove two hours to leave a note and some comforting gifts on our front porch to encourage us. We still have the bottle of Maker's Mark bourbon he left for us that day. The label is charred from our fire—it's a treasure we were grateful to retrieve from the rubble.

I had to face the reality that I'd been part of starting a church that was hurting people. It was doing a lot of good things, too. That's what made it all so complicated and crazy. Many grew and learned there and more fully became who they'd been created to be. They were taught by inspiring preachers. They learned to parent and to steward their finances. Marriages were strengthened and healed. College students were discipled.

Moving Toward Freedom

It was important for me to walk as I listened to the *Mars Hill* podcast and considered the eerie similarities to my experience. Movement provided a way of discharging my nervous system.

Van der Kolk has noticed patients who have experienced various types of distress or trauma often "discover powerful physical impulses," and pairing movement with processing difficult memories can help heal them.[5]

It breaks my heart to realize that the church is associated with that kind of suffering for me and others. Yet there is healing power in talking about the toxic cultures that sometimes thrive in communities, worship and otherwise. Another Austin pastor said the stories of the fallout from Mars Hill helped her realize she's "not a weak or bad person for having been part of a dysfunctional system." And it helped her feel less alone knowing others have survived abusive church systems. She could take responsibility for her unwitting participation in things that hurt others even as she recognized she wasn't the one proactively harming others. She could mourn what was lost and how she'd been wounded by the dysfunction.

I bounced between fury and shame anytime I thought of those leaders for many years. I felt like a fool to have missed patterns that seemed so clear in retrospect. I was also outraged; I was angry at the ways we had been manipulated. Furious at the way we'd been limited and shut down in subtle and overt ways. I couldn't stop wondering if I could have done more to advocate for health and healing. Some of my family and friends worried I was becoming bitter and jaded, that I'd never make peace with the church. Their concerns were valid. But it was part of my faithfulness to bring these things into the light. And that meant refusing to suppress my grief or my anger.

An essential part of healing these things is to shine a light on ugly realities so a different way forward can become clear.

I'll be forever grateful for those who listened and validated my experiences in those days. My spiritual director encouraged me to try a compline service at a beautiful, historic Episcopal church near my home. She told me I could sit quietly in the back, and that no one would talk to me. It was exactly what I needed at the time. It sparked a measure of healing to quietly participate in a simple evening prayer service where I could be anonymous.

You might need to give yourself permission to take a break for a time from church or the kind of community where you experienced harm. You might join a book club. Or you could try attending services online or with a community of a different size, style, or denomination. You might gather with those of another culture or language. You can feel free to stay in the back row, go to the potluck without bringing a dish, or offer to make coffee or work in the nursery instead of signing up to greet other newcomers. Whatever you do, go kindly and be patient with yourself as you heal and rebuild.

Many who leave toxic organizations believe they deserved how they've been treated. That they are hopelessly broken and can never measure up. DeGroat contends, "Those who ascend [to be empowered as leaders] tend to collude with the system. Those who ultimately refuse to idealize the leader are chewed up and spit out."[6] A friend who is a therapist told me that abusive systems forcefully communicate "don't see, don't feel, and don't speak." Because the name of God is attached in a ministry setting, brokenness often goes unquestioned.

As I tried to make sense of what had happened, I learned many counselors in my city were helping former members heal an image of God as harsh and vengeful. I sought counseling myself for help repairing harm in God's name, to which childhood abuse and trauma had primed me to be vulnerable.

It took years to receive forgiveness from God and myself for my role in creating a church that had hurt so many. I thought a lot about how Jesus said it's better to put a millstone around your neck and be plunged into deep waters than to cause little ones to stumble (Luke 17:2). I was exhausted, heartbroken, and weighed down with grief and guilt.

I felt the weight of precious souls scarred. I feel it still even though I no longer carry it alone. Jesus' gentle way really is easier (Matthew 11:29-30). I've asked for forgiveness from former members wherever possible. One woman told me honestly that she considered me partially responsible for her harsh treatment while she was on staff. I'd urged her to take the job to foster support for women in ministry and encourage a humbler posture among leaders. I promised I'd advocate for her. And I tried my best. But I couldn't protect her from harm. I needed to take responsibility for that. Thankfully, she forgave me, and we remain close friends to this day.

And I reached out to the woman I encouraged to be more forgiving and trusting of leaders who she knew were being manipulative, but she never replied. I respect her right to maintain distance; I failed her and many others profoundly.

Through it all God didn't let me or my family go. Our wounds healing, we found a small liturgical community where we felt welcome to be where we were. I didn't have to paste on a smile. It was quiet and simple. I'll always be grateful for the way that community welcomed us.

Reading about these painful events may have surfaced similar experiences in your history in a church, community, or workplace. Bessel van der Kolk says it is important to focus on thoughts and physical sensations in moments of disquiet. He urges patients to "focus on that sensation and see how it changes when you take a deep breath out, or when you tap your chest just below your collarbone, or when you allow yourself to cry."[7] He's describing practices that have been shown to improve all sorts of stress-induced physical and emotional symptoms as well as foster healthier "immune response, blood pressure, and cortisol levels."[8]

I encourage you to pause and give one of his suggestions a try. Try breathing out deeply and audibly. Tap your chest gently. Let tears come if they're just under the surface. Notice how your shoulders feel after rolling them a few times; maybe you'll hear cracks and pops when you do. You are safe enough in this moment. You are beloved of God. And there is more life and wholeness on the other side of engaging subjects like these with empathy and honesty.

Complex Wounds and Secrets

The church my family had given so much life and love to left me and others with layers of wounds, but I didn't feel free to talk about them. At dinner with a fellow church planter a few years later, I kept choking on my salad as I tried to tell her my story. My throat was constricting as anxiety manifested physically. I had a coughing fit during my first semester of seminary when the professor started talking about the suppression of women's ministry in the Western church. I had to leave the room to get my bearings. I chalked it up to a coincidence—*surely it was just my allergies*—at the time. Now I know that the pain and grief of my ministry history that lived in my body and soul were getting surfaced. It is no coincidence it was making it physically impossible to speak.

Along the way, my first spiritual director once pointed out how I studiously avoided naming the leaders whose behavior had caused so much harm. He'd noticed a similar reservation in others that seemed more than discretion. My subsequent spiritual director and, later my therapist, noticed my reticence as well.

We'd been told repeatedly that to talk with outsiders about any negative aspects of the church is gossip. The implication was that it is a betrayal of the leaders, the community, and even God. But that fear of retribution is being worked out of me. I'm in the process of shedding the false belief that telling the truth about oppressive and exploitive practices and systems is wrong. In fact, it's faithfulness to a God who loves the least and who promises judgment to any who use their power to hurt.

I believed I was responsible to keep bad behavior a secret, even to others' and my harm. The truth is that what happened—good and bad—matters. DeGroat says his experiences of narcissistic abuse left him "feeling small, powerless, terrified, crazy, exasperated, enraged, and ashamed."[9] If you've been through anything similar, you need to know you're not crazy, exaggerating, or alone.

I've cried over the destructive choices of the leaders I served with. Those men were once beloved brothers—exasperating and annoying at times, but friends. I've mourned the brokenness we once recognized and worked together to heal; I've grieved the ways harmful things were insidiously reborn under their watch. I've sobbed for those crushed by their leadership. I've cried for what might have been.

And I've prayed they would be held accountable. I've asked that they'd awaken to their belovedness, recognizing their worth isn't tied to sermon downloads, members, or campuses. Over time and with grace, I have forgiven. I have compassion for their unhealed wounds. I see the training and systems that colluded with the worst parts of them. And yet the ongoing consequences of their actions matter.

If you have been part of causing that kind of harm for another in your church, family, or community, intentionally or not, I hope you'll allow yourself to mourn it so restoration can begin. Have the courage to make a fresh start, since that's what repentance truly is. Do your utmost to make amends with those you've hurt even as you recognize, as I had to, that some won't be able to give you second, third, or hundredth chances.

When Church Is a Trigger

I'm still convinced a resurrected God is somehow mystically present among us, loving people to life and drawing us into more of God's good ways. I believe there is always a faithful remnant even when dysfunction exists. But even though I love the church and have received God's love and goodness in it, it has nearly destroyed me. It has sometimes been like a parent who left me beaten and bruised too many times. One who is always sorry and promises to do better later.

And that has meant worship spaces sometimes feel unsafe for me. Contemporary worship music, some cadences of preaching, and sanctuaries with dimmed lights occasionally spark anxiety for me. Trauma creates physical changes in the nervous system influencing how risk and safety are perceived.

My first panic attack in a worship setting was at a weekend worship conference. Two men performed a worship song to close our time. I'd never heard it before. The music and lyrics were beautiful. But the cadence of the music, the repetitions of the chorus, and its slowly building crescendo felt disturbingly familiar. I started feeling off. As the music swelled, my body got cold, and I felt a weight on my chest. I tried to stay calm, pressing my palms to the polished wood of the pew. But I had to get out of the room. And even when I was catching my breath on the sidewalk outside, my heart kept pounding.

Hearing that song in a beautiful sanctuary lined with stained-glass windows, painful memories were surfaced below my conscious awareness. The churchiness of my environment and the weight of grief and trauma connected with it got stirred up without me realizing it was happening.

The trappings of that style of worship music got wrapped up with my experiences of pain, grief, and toxicity in the church. Daniel Siegal says, "What fires together, wires together."[10] Therapist Gena St. David says our brains start responding to our environments and fire in ways creating "felt emotions and sensations in our body *prior* to us arriving at an explanation or story about what has occurred."[11]

Van der Kolk says helping trauma survivors reset so that their survival mechanisms stop overfunctioning is essential for healing. This involves cultivating appropriate responses to danger, and even more importantly regaining "the capacity to experience safety, relaxation, and true reciprocity."[12]

A doctor who treats anxiety says that "people have the idea that panic attacks come out of nowhere, but they don't. . . . The body gets the message that something is wrong, and it builds up to a panic attack" in which muscles tighten, hearts pound, and breath gets constricted.[13] Typically, one or more incidents contribute. My nervous system had started getting stirred up the night before and slowly built to my overwhelming anxiety during that last song.

Habakkuk describes how anxiety can manifest physically. "I hear, and I tremble within; my lips quiver at the sound. Rottenness enters into my bones, and my steps tremble beneath me" (Habakkuk 3:16). That verse is just before the prophet's often quoted words about rejoicing in the Lord even in times of scarcity, when "the fig tree does not blossom" (Habakkuk 3:17). Here again, the Bible tells the truth about suffering. There is good reason to trust that goodness and mercy will return. But the biblical narrative consistently resists our temptations to bypass pain.

Confession and Healing Shame

Diane Langberg contends, "Forgiveness of any wrong, let alone a life-shattering one, is never a 'just do it' task."[14] The goal is not to forget but to rebuild and restore. And that takes time and willingness to feel pain and move through it. It requires courage to acknowledge harm that was hidden in plain sight and any unwitting participation in damaging patterns.

When I lead lament workshops, people usually arrive expecting to encounter sadness or tears. They are often surprised by their anger. Claire Bidwell Smith says grieving clients frequently disappoint themselves by lashing out at store clerks or delivery drivers. Her suggestion is not to excuse outbursts, while understanding "a short fuse can be expected."[15]

A sense of frustration at loss, missed opportunities, and injustice is just as acceptable as sadness. Neither grief nor anger are too much for the Divine. The God who roared in outrage at nations who oppressed their neighbors and the one who turned over tables in the temple has plenty of capacity for the full range of your emotions. He welcomes anger at suffering and injustice and even joins us in it. God gets mad at oppression, and our anger at injustice can even operate like praise (Psalm 76:7-10).

Survivors often worry they won't be believed or that their experience will be minimized, especially if the accused is a pastor or religious leader. Sadly, they are often right. One man's abusive youth pastor was fired, but the senior pastor told the man firmly, "If you want to be faithful, you will be quiet."[16] Church leaders didn't go to the police, offer the victim care, or warn other churches.

Remaining silent doesn't serve those who have been maltreated, only those who gain from the status quo. That doesn't mean talking about abuse and dysfunction will be easy, but it is an essential part of beginning to heal it. Holocaust survivor Elie Wiesel said, "Neutrality always helps the oppressor, never the victim. Silence encourages the tormenter, never the tormented."[17]

Jesus refused to accept religion that privileged the powerful at the expense of the defenseless. It's vital to acknowledge where systemic harm and oppression have existed, lament the damage fully, and then act courageously toward restoration. Bringing bad behavior or dysfunctional patterns into the light is painful and costly. Some will accuse you of holding on to resentments or being vengeful. And while those real temptations must be resisted, speaking about damage is part of healing.

I think I understand who is to blame now, when women like me have failed to live into the fullness of our gifts. We all are—God, forgive us. We didn't know what we were doing. When Jesus prayed like that from the cross, he didn't mean people were unaware he was dying. He meant they had reframed why it was happening and who was responsible. I was complicit in the marginalization of women in my communities even as I was hurt by it. I let myself be seen as exceptional because it meant I was allowed to participate in ministry leadership. I failed my community, women *and* men, every time I did.

But it wasn't just women like me. Modern-day Pharisees have preferred to keep deciding who gets grace and who doesn't. Some of them would rather healing doesn't happen if it won't fit their norms. Father, forgive them. Many don't know what they were doing. I don't mean that those who misuse their power or authority to benefit themselves, or ignore it when others do, aren't culpable. But I recognize that many have been misled by theologians and leaders they trust and have been blind to the consequences.

Beginning to pray for wrongdoers to receive God's love and kindness shifts something in us and has the power to unlock grace for them. And it just might lead to them finding the courage to face the harm they've allowed to perpetuate. Either way, it frees us to live honestly and without bitterness.

I wonder, Where do you hold yourself back from joy, grace, or purpose? Wherever you tend to minimize your abilities or err toward self-importance and pride, there is an invitation to turn toward freedom. And that starts with the necessary work of telling yourself the truth about what is, where responsibility lies (other's and your own), and what more wholeness looks like.

Lament is the courage to face the beautiful as well as the broken. Diana Butler Bass describes it as the need for both priestly and prophetic faith, combining religious expressions that honor the past with prophetic expressions that speak to the moment in a way that "holds the nation accountable to God's standards and judgments."[18] Prophetic voices will make us uncomfortable at times. That is part of the difficult goodness of faithful lament.

The authors of *Forgive Us* invite the American evangelical church to acknowledge the ways our history includes patterns of sin against creation, indigenous peoples, African Americans and other people of color, women, the LGBTQ+ community, immigrants, Jews, and Muslims. They maintain, "The church often allows our congregations either to ignore lament altogether or to move as quickly as possible past confession and lament toward praise and celebration. They treat confession as merely a stepping stone."[19] The impact of the long absence of genuine confession and faithful lament in many of our communities is profound. Healing must be an overflow of acknowledging blind spots. We have a lot to reckon with.

Alexia Salvatierra and Peter Heltzel say Moses learned two things at the burning bush. He discovered, "God's most personal and precious name, and God's most earnest message of liberation for the oppressed."[20] Nicholas Wolterstorff describes oppression as the impairment of shalom in the face of a God who wants every creature to flourish. He contends, "Love and justice are not pitted against each other but are intertwined."[21]

We can choose to care about what God cares about. We can notice how habitually God sides with the weak and marginalized. For those in positions of more relative power, lament may be invited around harmful choices, and those in positions of less power may need to grieve damage and the sense of powerlessness at the hands of others or by corrupt systems. Most of us have areas of privilege and areas where we are marginalized, which means many of us will need to engage some confessional and some healing laments.

These kinds of laments rarely remain individual, even though their work begins in solitary hearts and souls. I wonder what it looks like for us to corporately lament over the state of communities and organizations and the abuse and injustice that are sometimes allowed to fester within them.

Energy for healing and change won't come if we're stuck avoiding naming injustice because of grief, guilt, or shame. Faithful lament honors the need to process those things by speaking and enacting grief. Lament is a way to move through them, so they don't keep spiraling inside, hindering healing.

Biblical and modern laments are the opposite of surrendering to despair. Instead they are courageous ways of enacting grief and cries for justice, redemption, and restoration together "through which a community's suffering, mourning and hope are articulated."[22] Engaging lament can set individuals and peoples free, liberating us from the paralyzing effects of guilt and shame, which thrive when brokenness stays hidden, numbed, or repressed.

Grounding Practice

WHEN YOU ARE FEELING STRESSED OR ANXIOUS about daily life, what is happening in the world, or a complicated part of your history that has resurfaced, grounding in your body and your physical surroundings can be helpful.[1] Kolber suggests engaging exercises like these "when you begin to feel disconnected or overwhelmed to help you move back into your WOT [window of tolerance]."[2] Your WOT is your Goldilocks zone of not too much or too little stress. This practice has three movements. It takes around ten minutes to engage all three. If you're short on time, you can choose one or two.

There are a few things to keep in mind before you begin. Menakem says that during or soon after engaging a mind-soul-body practice like this, "it's possible your body may have an unusual reaction. You might start shaking or tingling; you might laugh or cry, or burp or fart, or feel hot or cold. You may feel an impulse to move your body in a particular way."[3] He adds you might also have an unexpected image, thought, or emotion. Know that all of these things are completely normal. However, if you begin to feel anxious or respond in a negative way to the exercise, simply stop and focus on your breath.

Start this practice by looking around you, including above and behind you. As you look, pay attention to your surroundings.

Then begin scanning your body starting at the top of your head. Move slowly down your head, neck, and shoulders, noticing sensations. Continue to your back and belly, your hips and thighs, your calves and so on, all the way to your toes.

Are there places in your body that feel light, free, and energized? Are there other places where you feel tension or pain? Are there parts of your body that feel numb or vacant?

If there is a place of particular sensation, you could try placing a hand on that part of your body. You could even experiment with speaking kindly to your body. Kolber encourages saying something like "thank you for telling me this" to your body. If you're anything like me, that might feel a little silly at first. I encourage you to try it anyway and notice what happens.

Next, let your senses connect with your physical space. Do this by noticing

- Five things you can see.
- Four things you can touch and touch them.
- Three things you can hear.
- Two things you can smell. Feel free to move around the room.
- One thing you can taste. It might be a lingering flavor from your coffee or tea, your lunch, or something else.

Last, scan your body again. Start at the top of your head and slowly make your way to the tips of your toes. Notice your posture, your breathing, and the feeling of your clothing against your skin. Pay attention to "warmth, coolness, relaxation, tightness, softness, pressure, energy, numbness."[4] Has anything shifted since your first body scan?

Body Practice for Children and Families

For this practice, and for all practices with children, I encourage you to welcome a playful posture in your own soul and with them. It's perfectly okay for this to be lighthearted or to be more contemplative. Let the children set the tone, showing you what they need for the day. If they are processing hard events or emotions, be prepared for an interplay of anger and sadness with laughter and happiness. This doesn't mean the child isn't taking things seriously. They can attend almost simultaneously to the humor of holding and acting out these postures, and their sadness or frustration.

In that, as in so many other things, the children among us can become our teachers if we let them. Lacy Finn Borgo tells the story of a young boy who was mad at his brother and acted out his prayer. She wrote that he "stood up, widened his arms and squatted like a gorilla," praying "Watch me, this is how I feel, God!"[5] Such embodied and enacted prayers can be healing in more ways than one.

Have a soft blanket, yoga mat, or another comfortable space to lie down or spread out on the floor for this activity if possible. Invite the child to let their body make a shape that tells how they feel. You might join them and let your body do the same. Invite them to stay in that posture for three to five breaths or longer.

Next, invite the child to let their body take a shape that tells God what they hope or what they need. Again, I encourage you to consider joining them and letting your body take a similar posture.

Finally, invite the child to add some movement to their shape. It might be stretching their arms above their heads, wiggling their toes, jabbing the air with their fists, or making a "floor angel" on the ground.

8

Grieving Together

Lord God, mercy is in your hands, pour me a little. And tenderness, too. My need is great.

MARY OLIVER

WE LEARNED TOREY was expecting her first child in late summer. I was thrilled for my daughter and her husband to become parents. Since I grew up with sisters I was delighted and a little mystified about welcoming a baby boy. Psychotherapist Sylvia Boorstein describes parenting as mortgaging your heart for the rest of your life. She says it's incredible to "create a new life that comes out with fingernails and eyelashes and all its fingers and toes. . . . And it's extremely awakening, in the sense of knowing how vulnerable we are."[1] Conception during a pandemic worried my mama's heart, but they were careful and wise. I took it as a chance to pray even more intentionally. Nothing clouded the joy of his existence.

The impulse to intercede got more urgent during her twelfth week. Near the end of a routine screening, the doctor abruptly stated something was wrong. An alert from our family's group text popped up on my screen as I led an online training. It was a moment when cameras were off as the students did some reflective writing. I read a stark message: "Our baby has a bowel obstruction or cystic fibrosis." My belly dropped. I typed a prayer and said I didn't know of any family history of the condition. They had more questions, of course. I promised to call as soon as I finished with my students. We were mercifully almost done with our last session.

After breathing another prayer, I returned my attention to the training. My presence was split as I felt anxiety about the baby alongside care for the important work the spiritual direction students were doing. After our time closed, I spent a few minutes tending my worries with God. Then I searched for *cystic fibrosis*, since it was a disorder I knew little about. My eyes filled with tears as I read that a life span of less than forty years is common.

I grabbed a few prayer tools and headed to Torey and Craig's home. He was on the phone with the doctor who was patiently answering his questions. I am grateful for medical practitioners who understand their job is more than diagnosing and treating bodies. Torey was out for a walk, listening to Rich Mullins's "Hold Me Jesus," a song we'd listened to often when she was young. I think the lines were becoming a new kind prayer for her that day.

Together, we read about the Spirit of God hovering over the waters of creation. The Hebrew word רוּחַ (*ruah*) can mean spirit, wind, or breath. *Ruah* appears to "belong to the category of onomatopoeic words . . . [imitating] the sound of the whistling wind and excited breathing."[2] Try whispering it to yourself and you'll hear why linguists reached that conclusion. The idea of God's Spirit moving unseen, enlivening creation like wind over a chaotic sea, is precious to me. That we live filling our lungs invisibly with the breath of life is similarly sacred.

In the creation narrative, as for most of its appearances in the Old Testament, *ruah* is feminine, so thinking of the Spirit as a mothering *She* is fitting.[3] Julian of Norwich was a mystic who taught about encountering God as Mother *and* Father. She wrote, "God almighty is our loving Father, and God all wisdom is our loving Mother, with the love and goodness of the Holy Spirit, which is all one God, one Lord."[4] We were in desperate need of that kind of loving maternal Presence. We sat quietly holding our own worries alongside our concern for each other and the baby in Torey's womb.

In the days of uncertainty ahead, I found solace in an unmistakable sense that whatever physical challenges he had, my grandson was safe in God's love. The idea that as he was growing inside his mama's womb he was held in what John of the Cross called the "luminous darkness" of the Spirit's presence, had been with me ever since I'd first seen his tiny features in a sonogram.[5]

A few days later, as we exchanged heartfelt prayers in our family's group text, a bright "Hello!" appeared in the middle of the interchange. Torey quickly wrote, "Sorry accidental watch text." Technology is a strange miracle. We were talking about the life of a beloved child from separate locations amid our daily activities, with the odd comic relief of an automated greeting in the middle of it all. We are in a time in which many of us need to splinter attention between digital and physical spaces. There is no question that the ability to connect remotely comes with benefits.

But the costs of that kind of fragmentation are also real. Which means that it's vital to take time away from technology to engage embodied restorative physical activities like the sacred practices they are. Things like walking, stretching, cycling, yoga, or simply taking deep and intentional breaths are essential for all of us.

Beloved Baby Isaiah

A month later, our family was scattered in different locations again. I'd just sat down to dinner after a long day of work when another devastating text appeared. Torey was visiting Craig's parents, and they were rushing her to the hospital. Kyle was waiting for a flight home from a business trip, but it wasn't for a few hours.

Reeling, I packed a bag and waited for Craig to arrive so we could make the drive to Houston. I paced, cried, and prayed. My prayer was mostly a single word. "No! Please God, no." It was equal parts angry demand and despairing plea. Torey was past the point when miscarriage was a significant risk. But she was losing baby Isaiah.

She started bleeding heavily after they arrived in the ER. She could hear another woman wailing in pain and anguish through her *eleventh* pregnancy loss. When Torey's mother-in-law, Denise, asked if she was going to be okay, the doctor replied, with terrifying honesty, that she didn't know; she explained miscarriage was inevitable and that Torey might need surgery.

As Craig and I sped east, Denise kept us informed, telling us they were giving Torey blood and that she was resting some. She reassured us her vitals were steady and that this was some version of normal under the hateful circumstances. She had also experienced the pain of miscarriage and lovingly stayed at Torey's elbow, whispering prayers and psalms before we arrived.

My beloved daughter remembers everything hurting, as Covid tests were shoved up her nose and IV catheters pierced her hands. She saw the panic in the eyes of the nurses. She also saw them recover quickly and offer her steadfast care and comfort. One of them, a Nigerian American woman, talked about losing her own child. She told Torey how she had had another baby soon after. She talked about the story of Anna meeting Jesus in the temple and how hope and joy can follow loss.

Craig and I finally made it to the hospital after the longest three-hour drive of our lives. We held Torey's hands as we learned surgery would be necessary. Mercifully, the shift had ended for the doctor who curtly expressed doubts about Torey's well-being. A much gentler doctor explained the procedure and its potential risks.

The kindhearted nurse who'd talked about Anna, gently pressed Torey's hand in its nest of plastic tubes and then squeezed Denise and me tightly. We stumbled into an elevator with Craig signing paperwork as surgical nurses wheeled Torey's bed inside and then to surgery upstairs.

And then we numbly waited and waited and waited in a bright and spacious lobby. The reality of losing Isaiah and the danger to Torey's life were becoming more real to each of us as the minutes ticked by. I sipped a cup of weak coffee as we sat quietly, praying to ourselves. I paced as Craig fell into a merciful doze. I was fighting an irrational impulse to crash through the emergency doors to get to where my daughter and grandson were.

After an hour that felt like an eternity, the doctor returned to tell us Torey was well and safe. A nurse led Craig to sit with her as she woke up. He texted Denise and me that he'd seen the monitor show her heartrate slowing dramatically when she realized he was there.

Exhausted nurses guided us to a room where Torey could settle in for the night, gently helping her move from the stretcher to a bed as she groggily thanked them. In those moments and throughout, I was amazed by Torey's courage and her kindness to all who were helping her.

I helped her wash her face and brush her teeth, then tucked a soft blanket I grabbed on the way out the door under her chin. I wrapped myself in the sheet a thoughtful nurse had brought me and pulled a chair close to her bed, settling in to keep watch. Torey dozed, frequently startling awake reliving the horrors of the previous hours.

There were mercies within excruciating, unspeakable loss. It's a grace that Torey was with her beloved mother-in-law instead of on a plane, as she'd been mere hours before. There is lovingkindness in the fact that blood was available when she needed a transfusion. We experienced the gift of skilled doctors and caring nurses working the night shift.

Healing Gently Together

When we returned home, Torey and Craig received an outpouring of love. In times of uncertainty there is power in simply being with those experiencing it, as well as in providing or sharing meals.

The Jewish practice of shiva is a great picture of grieving in community. Close family members gather, cover mirrors, and dress simply to convey a lack of attention to appearance. They sit on or near the floor to convey being brought low in grief.[6] Friends and family sometimes simply bring meals or other comforts, and other times sit with those mourning, holding the grief with them for a time. Job and his friends modeled shiva in the first days of his losses as they sat with him in silence with garments torn and ashes in their hair, communing in the magnitude of his losses in physical ways.

Friends and family shared their experiences of pregnancy losses, and Torey and Craig began to understand the extent to which they were not alone. But that didn't make the death of their beloved child any less devastating.

In the days ahead, they grieved faithfully, together and on their own. They began healing without pretending to be anything other than heartbroken. They were like Rachel, bereft and aching: "A voice was heard in Ramah, wailing and loud lamentation, Rachel weeping for her children; she refused to be consoled, because they are no more" (Matthew 2:18). Rachel wailed for her pain and for children she couldn't see or comfort. She cried, as we did, because of loss that was real and profound. We wept for my daughter's achingly empty womb and for the child they would not hold, a precious life cut short.

A few days after my grandson's loss, the words "I am the resurrection and the life" were echoing in my mind (John 11:25).

I shot back at the Spirit, "So what? Where is he *now*?" I was heartbroken and angry God hadn't intervened.

I read the verse as a prayer at dinner that night, believing and asking God to help my unbelief. But it would probably have been better to have read what happened just after Jesus spoke those words, when he simply cried with all those who had lost Lazarus (John 11:33-35).

Questioning Like Job

When you and your loved ones encounter pain or loss, it's a holy opportunity to reflect on God's presence and power in times of suffering, as Job did. He wasn't afraid to ask God if he'd fallen asleep on the job; he called out his friends for their cold comfort; and he steadfastly rejected the assumption that all suffering is deserved.

His friends were scandalized that he dared suggest his pain was anything except punishment. They used the same kinds of truisms, false certainties, and avoidance those enduring suffering often hear today. Eliphaz assured Job that after he endured divine retribution things would undoubtedly get better. Bildad said his children were the real villains, but that he should focus on getting happy again anyway. Zophar scolded Job for bragging about his faithfulness and prodded him to hurry up and confess.

They were all completely confident and utterly wrong. Thomas Kelly said, "God's love isn't just a diffused benevolence."[7] It is as particular as our griefs, our needs, our longings. And we can both receive our portion of divine love and do our part to be a channel of it for others,[8] which is the furthest thing from what Job's friends did.

They denied the possibility of innocent suffering, even when it was literally staring them in the face. In Diane Glancy's poem, Job's daughters bear witness from the grave, declaring "The friends, Eliphaz, Bildad, Zophar, will hit our father / when he is down . . . footnoting him to death."[9] Their words were adding to his suffering, and Job was finished debating them, dreaming of questioning God directly instead.

Brueggemann says Western culture, including much of the church, is just as susceptible to denial as Job's friends. He argues, "A church that goes on singing 'happy songs' in the face of raw reality is doing something very different from what the Bible itself does."[10] We are allowed to admit when it seems darkness is winning.

When the poet Ann Weems lost her twenty-one-year-old son, she wrote a psalm of lament, telling God,

> You are the power:
> Why didn't you use it?
> You are the glory,
> but there was no glory in his death.[11]

Ann felt Job's freedom to complain and ask God hard questions about suffering. She felt permission to weep, knowing her son's loss was a wound impossible to fully heal this side of heaven.

Grieving Together, Separately

Adriel Booker says she started understanding Old Testament practices of tearing clothes and smearing on ashes in a new way following her miscarriage, since those things "would have felt entirely appropriate as an external outworking of my internal anguish and lament."[12] In the awful aftermath of her fourth pregnancy loss, all she wanted to do was tear off her clothes and curl up on the ground. A beloved family member who experienced two miscarriages in quick succession explained not wanting to talk about the losses, alongside the excruciating reality that they were all she could think about.

Torey was given a copy of Booker's guide for moms who have lost children—it was a lifeline. Booker invites grieving parents to write themselves a letter giving permission to feel everything they feel as it is (instead of what they might wish it was), noticing what threatens to short-circuit grieving, and considering help they need to grieve well. Help might look like sharing the story of the loss, mental health support, or being honest with partners about how the death is impacting them.[13] She urges parents to simply start writing, letting the answers unfold. Whatever you are facing, I wonder what you would write if you sent yourself such a letter. You could also write to God, pouring out questions and asking for help.

Dr. Sarah Philpott acknowledges how hard it can be to know what to say to someone who is bereaved.[14] Mistaken explanations and other hurtful responses to loss abound. It's vital that grieving parents reject careless or ill-informed judgments on top of the loss they are enduring. Philpott emphasizes most pregnancy loss is caused by chromosomal abnormalities and *not* anything like heavy lifting, exercise, or stress.

She also says, "Minimizing halts recovery."[15] Trite responses like "It was God's will," "At least it happened early," and "Why don't you just adopt?" compound grief. And it can be just as harmful when people avoid talking about the loss.

If children are mourning alongside you, it adds extra layers of grief and complexity. Dr. Philpott urges parents to simply and honestly tell children what happened. Even young children can understand something like, "The baby that was growing in my belly died. We are very sad."[16] Welcome children's questions and know they will have different emotional processes than you will. Create as much hospitality for all as you can. Extended family and friends can be an important support when you need to tend to your grief individually. Reach out for help as you need!

Khris Ford says that families grieving together are like riding a merry-go-round, with each person moving in and out of mourning in their own ways.[17] Every person has a unique way of expressing grief. There isn't one right way to mourn. For some, bereavement looks like tears, while it's expressed through activity for others. One family member may find talking about the loss helpful, while for another it is too painful. Some loving negotiation will probably be required. Honoring each person's way of expressing sorrow helps you all to move through loss together. If you have experienced a loss that is often unseen or minimized, please be gentle with yourself and with those experiencing it with you as you heal.

Mandala Practice

A MANDALA IS A CIRCLE OR EGG that represents wholeness. Artists, retreat leaders, and spiritual directors Christine Valters Paintner and Betsey Beckman say the mandala is "a sacred form used in many traditions as a tool for centering and prayer."[1]

You might consider it a way of holding together lament and hope. What are you grieving? Where is the flame of hope burning bright or flickering dimly? What possibilities for reconnection, renewal, or wholeness can you sense?

The eleventh century Benedictine abbess and mystic Hildegard of Bingen saw visions of God, heaven, and humanity that often appeared in the form of mandalas. She saw the universe, with all its beauty and wonder, as well as the horrors of evil and judgment, as "a vast instrument, round and shadowed, in the shape of an egg, small at the top, large in the middle and narrowed at the bottom; outside it, surrounding its circumference, there was bright fire . . ."[2]

To make your own mandala, gather some supplies like art paper or a journal, paper for tearing and/or using in collage, paint or markers, and tape or glue. This doesn't have to be complicated; use what you have on hand. You can use a circular object to trace your mandala, or you can draw your egg or circle freehand, welcoming any imperfections.

As with any creative practice like this, the goal is not to create an artistic masterpiece. Rather, it is to allow the practice to surface what you are sensing, praying, and hoping. I started a mandala journal last year and have found it a profound way to connect with both lament and hope. I have created mandalas to meditate on the words of mystics, on poems, on psalms of protest and complaint, on love, and on loss.

For your mandala, you could bring a passage of Scripture or a poem to reflect on and inspire your creation or you can simply trust your instincts and start drawing or painting, allowing your thoughts, emotions, and words to flow freely through color, texture, and images.

Once you've completed your mandala, I encourage you to include the date and journal about the experience. Notice what images stand out; what colors, shapes, and textures are reflected and what are they communicating? What has stayed hidden and what is made clearer? Is the surface covered or did you leave some open spaces? Is your work contained within the edges of the mandala or did your design extend to the edges of the page?

In all of this, notice your emotions, memories stirred, and your sense of hope or of the presence of the Spirit.[3] Where are you in all of this? Has anything shifted for you?

Mandala-Making Practice for Children and Families

Children often enjoy creating mandalas, too. You can invite them to draw or collage their mandalas.

You could also gather materials like leaves, rocks, and feathers on a nature walk and create a mandala somewhere outside. The possibilities for playful presence and creativity abound. You could collaborate to create a mandala together or each create your own.

Once they've drawn, painted, collaged, or built their mandalas, talk about the colors and shapes used. What story are those colors and textures telling? Ask kids what they noticed in their bodies as they were making their mandala. Wonder with the children how their feelings were present and if they changed. You could also wonder with them about what God might be thinking about their mandala.

9

Children and Loss

God, can you hear me calling out?
Listen to me,
I'm crying for you!

MARIE-HELENE DELVAL

ONE OF MY EARLIEST MEMORIES is the day my dad moved out. I was three or four years old. I don't remember him loading his car or driving away. I don't recall much about living with him, just a few snapshots, like mom and him standing in our kitchen with the dark brown cabinets.

I didn't understand that he was gone and wasn't coming back, but I knew my mom was distraught. I felt guilty asking why she was upset, as if that would make it worse—and it seemed to when I did. She dropped the harvest gold hamper she was holding, dumping clean laundry in the hallway, and crumpled in tears. As a child, I believed if I hadn't let my curiosity get the better of me, she would have stayed happy.

It's not uncommon for children to feel responsible for the grief of significant adults in their lives. That can sometimes make kids reticent to share hard emotions with grownups.

Holly Catterton Allen, who has studied connections between children's spiritual formation and resilience, says, "Adults may not state explicitly how they are feeling in order to shield their children from their grief. The children may thus infer that talking about [the loss] is wrong or hurtful."[1]

I sensed my mom's palpable grief. And I missed my dad and wished I could see him and his parents more often. I'm far from alone in these experiences. In the United States, a million children a year have been impacted by the dissolution of their parents' marriage since the advent of no-fault divorce in 1973.[2] The rate of divorce remains around half of the marriage rate.[3] Allen says children with divorced parents are less likely to be religious than children with intact families.[4] She says they are "often deeply absorbed in their parents' needs and vulnerabilities; and they tend to confront complex moral questions earlier than their peers."[5] They also often feel less protected and cared for.

Grief is part of being human, but that doesn't prevent many of us from attempting to shield children from its reality. Western culture, especially the United States, is often "death-denying and grief-avoiding."[6] Children need our protection from harm and safeguarding from those who would wish them ill; but when pain or loss does happen, the best gift we can give them is to talk about it openly. Child psychologist David Walters argues that while it's meant to be protection from the harshness of the world, silence about suffering leaves children emotionally stunted and robs them of chances to work through it that can "furnish insight, adjustment, and healing."[7]

It's crucial to be honest with children about emotions in age-appropriate ways. Child psychologist Tobin Hart contends,

"The white or polite lie, the incongruence between what we say and how things are really going, fosters confusion instead of peace. Our being appropriately honest and congruent helps children to refine and trust their perceptions."[8]

When children experience loss, they tend to "grieve in bits and pieces."[9] For kids under five, sadness tends to be expressed through the body.[10] It might show up as stomachaches, bed-wetting, or another temporary regression. When my mom remarried, I started sucking my thumb again at night for a little while. Children coping in such ways need compassionate attention. Physical affection like hugs, sitting close for stories, and cuddles can be especially helpful.

Kids have limited emotional vocabularies and won't be able to stay with big emotions for long.[11] It's important to recognize that when kids swing from tears, anger, or grief to asking what's for dinner or laughing at a cartoon, it doesn't mean the loss isn't important to them. Younger children may struggle to comprehend the permanence of death. They may also worry they are responsible or that another bad thing is going to happen. Patiently hearing their concerns, often repeatedly, is essential. They also need permission to tell you when they don't want to talk about their grief.

For teens, it can be difficult to discern what is developmental and what is grief. D'Arcy and Ford encourage caregivers to watch for behavioral changes while honoring their intensified needs for privacy.[12] They also say anxiety, even more than sadness or anger, is often a primary emotion for grieving teens. It's important for adults to create "opportunities for children to safely ask their 'why' questions" which can moderate fear and anxiety.[13] Family, teachers, spiritual directors, and play therapists can make room for these to be surfaced. Being heard is part of healing.

Children need to understand their sorrows as much as adults do, but "the difference between adults and children lies in *how* and *when* they are able to make meaning of their loss."[14] Unlike most adults, kids don't compartmentalize their lives. Lacy Finn Borgo contends that for most children, there is "no secular or sacred."[15] Children need freedom to explore their griefs, joys, and questions at their own pace.

Old Enough to Grieve

A. D. Wolfelt says children are often "the forgotten mourners."[16] Children's grief matters, whether they are mourning major losses or grieving things like friends moving away or a broken keepsake. But children's questions about life and meaning are often dismissed in a version of "You're too young to understand." Tobin Hart says that when adults assume "spirituality is dependent on mature linguistic and rational capacities," it's more destructive than we realize.[17] Children grasp a lot about the spiritual world long before they can articulate it clearly.

When my family was leaving our church community, we were all grieving. As Torey talked about her sadness one day, I'm sorry to say I minimized her experience. I assumed it was somehow easier for her because she was younger. I'm glad she told me how hurtful my response was. She forgave me, but the harm was real. I missed a chance to be present with her suffering.

The truth is that grownups can learn about honest grief from the children among us. Kids are usually willing to admit what they don't know. They are learning to trust themselves and are often unafraid to ask for help. Jesus talked about children as ideal members of God's family (Mark 10:13-16). In his day, little ones were not idealized but seen as costly nuisances who got in the way—that's certainly how the disciples saw them. Jesus corrected his friends, telling them that God's ways belonged to those who were willing to be like children.

Someone who was a preschooler when "Baby Jessica" McClure fell down an abandoned well in West Texas, noticed grownups glued to the television as the little girl was trapped underground for three long days.[18] The child processed what was happening by playing with a friend, taking turns pretending to be stuck in a well like baby Jessica was. She and her friend were scolded and made to stop.

But playing is one way children make meaning. They weren't mocking or minimizing, but grappling with fear, danger, and hopes of rescue. That woman who once pretended to be stuck is now a play therapist. At the start of the pandemic, she gathered toys so her young sons could play their way to more understanding. She says it helped them work out their fears and questions. And since there was safety to express their perspectives, she also had a chance to correct misconceptions.

Shelly Melia is a children's pastor whose husband died suddenly when her kids were young. She says supporting children through loss can look like asking open-ended questions to understand their experience more completely, while assuring them "nothing they did caused the death."[19] She encourages caregivers to answer children's questions completely each time, understanding repetitive questions about grief reveal "they are trying to make sense of information they do not yet fully understand."[20]

Just as for adults, when children experience loss it often kindles reconsiderations of beliefs about life, death, and God. Melia encourages adults to include kids in worship and other ceremonies that can help them process things intergenerationally. And she urges expecting changes in their understandings over time, allowing "the depth of understanding of God to change as the child develops and experiences the loss in increasingly profound and complex ways."[21]

Sources of Grief for Children

Loss can take many forms, though some appear to assume "grief only occurs when a loved one dies."[22] Once, in a training for spiritual directors to offer holy listening with children, we talked about a variety of sources of grief for children. Our list included catastrophic events, environmental disasters, abuse, addiction, parental imprisonment, divorce, complex losses connected to the pandemic, war or violence, the loss of a pet, and the death of a loved one.

We also talked about ways that racism and other biases can hurt children. I mourn the reality that my two beloved African American godchildren will sometimes be unwelcome and endangered in ways I've never experienced as a white woman. My godson, who constantly draws and creates, loves to dance, and adores his little sister, heard the N-word before he was eleven. He's statistically more likely to be singled out as a troublemaker when he's out playing with friends. I pray he'll live a long and wonderful life, unlike twelve-year old Tamir Rice who was shot while playing in a park. I want my goddaughter who is strong, no-nonsense, and loves her big brother as fiercely as he loves her, to inherit a world that will welcome her instead of telling her to "go back where she came from."[23]

As we talked in the training, we surfaced school and other mass shootings as another cause for grief and anxiety among children. Jackie Baker, a specialist in children's social communication, says it's essential for caregivers to talk with kids about shootings when they happen. Hoping that they won't hear the news or trying to keep it from them are both unhelpful. She encourages parents to "take the child's lead," waiting to bring it up until they do, within reason.[24] If the child seems hesitant, we can remind them that they can talk to us about any worries. We can help them know who to approach if they feel unsafe and how important it is to speak up if they are concerned about a fellow student.

And too many kids are struggling with depression, anxiety, trauma, loneliness, and suicidal ideation, with children of color disproportionately at risk. The American Academy of Pediatrics and several other organizations issued a joint statement declaring a national emergency in child and adolescent mental health in 2021. They cited the pandemic, rising suicide rates, and more mental health–related ER visits.[25]

Suicide remains the second most common cause of death for children, adolescents, and young adults.[26] Young girls are more likely to attempt or commit suicide than boys.[27] And LGBTQ+ kids have the highest risk for contemplating, planning, and attempting suicide by a wide margin.[28] They're also much more likely to be bullied at school.[29] All these beloveds are made in God's image. Their suffering matters to God and to us.

If you sense that a child in your world might be feeling sad or depressed, ask them direct questions about how they're feeling or if they've ever considered hurting themselves. Experts say that far from putting ideas in their heads, such "questions can provide assurance that somebody cares and will give your child the chance to talk about problems."[30]

Accompanying Children in Grief

Good stories can help children cultivate resilience for enduring the hard alongside the beautiful in their worlds. Stories can help children nurture hope, transcend hard situations, gain insights into deeper realities, discover goodness and love, practice joy and peace, and confront fears.[31] When author Holly Catterton Allen reads a book with a child, she asks who they are in the story and if they have a favorite page.[32]

Children's author Kate DiCamillo was once asked whether books for young people should tell them the truth or preserve their innocence. She described a childhood friend who read *Charlotte's Web* repeatedly, not because she thought it would turn out differently but because she "knew that a terrible thing was going to happen, and . . . also knew that it was going to be okay somehow."[33] Kate's friend learned over repeated readings that she could hold the sadness alongside the love in the story. DiCamillo believes her job as a storyteller for children is telling the truth and making it bearable.[34]

When Sadness Is at Your Door, by Eva Eland, normalizes sadness as a natural part of living. She encourages kids to "try not to be afraid of Sadness. Give it a name. Listen to it. Ask where it comes from and what it needs."[35] Patrice Karst's *The*

Invisible String, Isabel Otter and Katie Rewse's *The Garden of Hope*, Lacy Finn Borgo's *All Will Be Well*, and Tomie dePaola's *Nana Upstairs & Nana Downstairs* address losing a loved one with tenderness and grace. Cynthia Rylant's *Dog Heaven* and Corrinne Averiss and Sebastian Pelon's *Hope* both honor the special relationship that children have with their pets. Margaret Holmes's *A Terrible Thing Happened* explores healing after traumatic events. And classic works of children's literature that address pain, loss, and growth like *Charlotte's Web*, *The Velveteen Rabbit*, *Bridge to Terabithia*, and The Chronicles of Narnia can all help children connect with their own experiences.

When I meet with children for spiritual direction, I sometimes ask them if they'd like to tell me a time when they experienced joy, fear, or sadness. Among the storytelling tools I offer is a set of figures from the Pixar film *Inside Out*. Many children enjoy using them to playfully tell their stories; Fear's plastic stand has broken off over time. I encourage you to get creative in helping the children in your life have space to tell their stories and feel their emotions. Simple tools like these figures can be helpful, but the best gift is your listening presence. Ask them if they will share a story of grief and loss, or happiness and hope with you. And then listen with love.

Paula D'Arcy talks about a bereaved family who kept a chart of emotions on their refrigerator along with magnets representing each family member.[36] Every morning they would place their magnets on the main emotion they were feeling. Practices like that communicate that all emotions, even difficult ones, are okay. And we can encourage children to feel free to bring their full selves into God's presence by modeling honest prayer and question-asking with them.

Adults can invite kids to draw their sadness or anger, choosing colors that express their feelings and moving the crayon or marker as slowly or fiercely as they want. Children can be encouraged to create or draw about losses, maybe drawing their family and adding a baby or grandparent who is in heaven.[37] Children may want to tell stories of their loved one or write a letter to God. You could also create a photo album together about the loss or the absent loved one. Making copies of photos or uploading them to photo books can keep them kid-friendly without endangering mementos. For young children, you could create a series of age-appropriate books with stories of a family member who has died. And tears are always welcome.

I once created a grief kit for children who lost a beloved grandparent, adding squishy balls to discharge anxiety and cloth for tearing. Because grief is sometimes experienced as anger, I also included some old dishes and safety googles to break the dishes with a hammer in a plastic tub (with supervision by caregivers, of course!). Other helpful items for a kid's grief kit are art watercolors and bubbles to blow out sadness and questions wordlessly.

You might invite kids to engage calming and centering practices. Valerie Hess and Marti Watson Garlett describe meditation as becoming like tea bags, "soaking deeply and quietly in God and his Word so that we can better hear him speak to our hearts and minds."[38] Children as young as four can engage meditation through taking a bubble bath while gazing at a calming picture or comforting phrase such as *God loves you* or *You are so loved* placed in view.[39]

Children also sometimes need help processing their existential questions around mystery and mortality. *What Is My Song?* describes a child's journey toward calling and belonging within an African village.[40] I once shared it with a child, who became distressed at the line "When I lay down to die." It surfaced his fears around the impermanence of life. My role was not to distract him with a happy thought, suppress his anxiety, or steer him toward what I thought he should take away, but to give his questions room to breathe. Because death is part of life, it is important to help children navigate questions and fears about it gently and honestly.

Lacy Finn Borgo contends adults are "often undone by the existential fears of children. A child's fears remind us of our own fears that we have worked hard to bury or rationalize."[41] She says they also remind us that we can't fix the larger world or solve the fears and worries of the children we love. Helping children tend ambiguity, uncertainty, and hard questions is part of our work as adults, even as we continue addressing them in ourselves. By cultivating more comfort with sadness and uncertainty, we become more resilient together.

Worry Tree Practice

FOR CHILDREN WHO ARE GRIEVING, the loss may surface worries that other things will go wrong. Invite the child or children to create a worry tree.[1] This can be drawing a tree on art paper and writing various worries as the leaves.

If the loss is more significant and invites more reflection over time, consider creating a tree trunk and limbs together out of butcher paper or wrapping paper. You can cut out leaves or simply use Post-it notes to serve as your tree's leaves. As often as helpful, invite the child or children to write down a worry and place it on the tree for safekeeping. Their worries might include things like: Will someone else get sick or hurt?, I am afraid I will forget the person we lost, or I worry I will always feel this sad. Assure the children that all worries are welcome and that nothing is off limits. Consider adding your worries to the tree in age-appropriate ways. Keep the tree available with resources to add more leaves as long as helpful.

Invite the children to let their worries become prayers if they'd like. You could read the following together: "O Most High, when I am afraid, I put my trust in you" (Psalm 56:2-3).

You could also read Psalm 23 or pray together after recording fears and anxieties.

A practice like this would work well in a community or worship setting following a loss or during Lent.

10

Finding the Way Through Lament

Let me learn, pang-by-pang,
O Lord, how these hurts—
while they will never in this life
completely cease—might serve like stitchings,
Binding me ever tighter to eternal hope.

DOUGLAS KAINE MCKELVEY

WE LOST OUR HOME, our vocations, and our community in a span of months. Other upheavals and significant losses unfolded over years. We'd heard one too many comparisons of our story with Job's. We were surviving—barely. We were depressed and shell-shocked. We got a little counseling. We healed some.

Kyle wrangled with our insurance agency until they corrected a critical error in our policy and the house got rebuilt. We decided to sell it and make a fresh start in a new part of town. We were looking for somewhere that could become home. Which matters to us because place matters to God. Cole

Arthur Riley says, "Isn't it something that in Genesis, God makes a home for things before God makes the thing? Not the fish first but the sea. Not the bird first but the sky. Not the human first but the garden."[1]

Doing (Some) Right Things

We considered a few neighborhoods. The day my husband and I were deciding whether to put an offer on what became our home, we rounded a bend past little league fields, arriving at a bridge over Lady Bird Lake. Gazing at the trees lining the shore and the peaceful water, I knew it was where I wanted to live.

But it was more than selecting a home in a favorite area of town. I had the sense moving there was the *right* thing to do. We were downsizing and moving to a more economically and racially diverse area, a few blocks from beloved godchildren. I'd always loved the idea of heaven being full of color and variety (Revelation 5:9), but except for a few brief periods I'd lived in suburban neighborhoods without much diversity. I was tired of communities filled with mostly white people. I wanted to put my money and home equity where my mouth was.

I was concerned about contributing to gentrification, but have worked hard to pay attention to and vote toward things like property tax relief for long-term residents. I've felt a mixture of concern and delight as fun but expensive new restaurants and shops have moved in. I wanted to be part of a neighborhood where we didn't sequester ourselves behind gates.

And my world is bigger now. I love the street art and that all the houses don't look alike. I love being able to call some of my unhoused neighbors by name. As I arrived at my block with takeout one afternoon, Marge and I smiled our hellos in the spring sun; I was glad to see her healthy and safe. I love the line snaking out of Juan in a Million's door every weekend. I appreciate the faith traditions, ethnicities, life stages, and families represented on our street. I enjoy living near the only historically African American university in the city. It's the campus where Howard Thurman gave a series of lectures in 1948 that became *Jesus and the Disinherited*.[2]

But while my family contributes to making our neighborhood warm and welcoming and caring, the benefits of our living here haven't accrued equally. Everything is getting more expensive. Whole Foods and Target have opened locations nearby. I've taken satisfaction at moving to a neighborhood former city leaders wanted to keep segregated, but I've been naive about the full impact of racism.

I don't believe it solves things for me to move back to the suburbs. If I leave my neighborhood, it won't make Austin any easier for the people most harmed by gentrification.

So I'm working to recognize my privilege and use it for others. I'm seeking to become more fully what Ibram X. Kendi calls an antiracist—a person who isn't simply not overtly racist but who is actively participating in healing what many have called America's original sin. Kendi says, "'Racist' and 'antiracist' are like peelable nametags [not] permanent tattoos."[3] I know all this is merely a beginning. Nothing built over this long can be fixed with an election, a bill, or a new friend made, though they all matter.

It's important to realize that racism is still insidiously within me, internalized because it's in the systems I've participated in as a southerner, cradle Baptist, and American. Intentionally or not, I am part of perpetuating things I say I hate. This isn't self-flagellation; it's simply recognizing that racism is more than people with evil intentions. Racism can be entrenched to such a degree that it doesn't require anyone who actively wishes people of color harm to continue causing injustice. Austin Channing Brown says, "Racism operates in systems and structures enabled by nice people."[4]

My invitation as a privileged white woman is to actively work to undo racism and other kinds of brokenness in and around me. Sometimes, lament must be the kind of repair that can only happen in community over time. The authors of *Forgive Us* contend, "A lament acknowledges reality and the necessity of repentance in response to that reality," resisting simplistic answers or quick fixes.[5] It's the only way forward that doesn't replay old harms or invent new ones.

Lament and Kindness

But as we settled into our new neighborhood, God was quiet. The silence started feeling deafening. Which was fine with me. I didn't have much to say to him, either. It had started feeling like God was mean. As if the Divine were harsh or vindictive. I wasn't motivated to do anything that had connected me with the Spirit before. No words came when I tried praying. I didn't want to read my Bible. Going to church felt impossible.

My faith felt broken. The still small voice I'd relied on all my life was silent—part of me wanted to stop hoping it would return. Not believing in God seemed more honest. I wondered if I was too much of a coward to admit that the One I'd spent my life loving, relating with, and inviting others to know wasn't real. It felt like I'd lost God. I wanted to give up. There were days back then when I just wanted to drive away, escaping to who knows where. On even darker days, I was tempted to find a cliff to drive off. Death seemed the best possible mercy.

Then one day, hope found me through a small, simple, and otherwise inconsequential decision. My friend Jenny had been beside me through it all, helping me not give up. She invited me for a day trip to a small town about an hour away. We chatted during the sunny drive, ate lunch, and looked at antiques. One shop had a collection of oversized metal paintings of Bible stories and saints, which had once hung in a European chapel, dating from the eve of the Second World War.

The one leaning against a wall in a back corner stopped me. It was of Jesus healing Jairus's daughter. She was ghostly pale, conveying how far gone she was. Her father and the disciples wear shocked expressions. Her mom is reaching for her daughter as tears dry on her cheeks. And Jesus is leaning to help the girl up with one hand while the other reaches for the mother's hand as he prepares to reunite them. But what captured me most was Jesus' face. His eyes looked gentle and full of compassion.

For the first time in years, I could imagine Jesus doing something other than judging or demanding. I could picture him doing something beyond telling people to get their acts together or being sovereign over suffering. The painting started shifting something in me that trying to force myself to pray or go to church couldn't. It reminded me of something familiar that I'd lost track of. This Jesus felt like a long-lost friend.

The story from the painting is in three of the four Gospels. Mark describes a crowd like rush hour at Grand Central. Word was getting around that Jesus was a healer and maybe even the Promised One, whatever that meant. So everywhere that Jesus went, the sick, the curious, the skeptics, and the people who wanted to see someone famous showed up. Mark says a religious leader named Jairus waded through the crowd because his daughter was dying. Jesus was his last hope. Jesus started weaving his way down the street shoulder-to-shoulder with a man trying to save a beloved child.

On the way, he stopped to comfort a woman who'd been sick for twelve years. She'd been in pain and ceremonially unclean that whole time, unable to worship with her people. Her last penny was spent on doctors, but she just got sicker. When she heard Jesus was in town, she took a chance. And as she touched his clothes, she got well; she knew it immediately. And Jesus felt it, too. He could have criticized her for making him unclean by touching him, but he praised her faith and celebrated her healing. I was starting to remember the Jesus who heals and speaks peace into people's lives.

But every minute counted with Jairus's daughter. While Jesus was talking, friends came to tell Jairus his daughter had died. They told him to leave the teacher alone. But Jesus told him not to be afraid, and they kept going toward Jairus's house.

When our house caught on fire, I was getting ready to take Kyle's parents to dinner at a restaurant with a beautiful view of Lake Travis. I had just pulled out my hair dryer when I heard my mother-in-law yelling. As black smoke poured into the kitchen and study, there was only time to help my in-laws get outside and grab my purse and our dog. Kyle, stuck in rush-hour traffic, called our friend who lived nearby. Doug came as fast as he could. I don't think he said anything. He just hugged me. He was one of hundreds of people who dropped everything and showed up to be with us that day and the ones that followed. They came to help. But mostly they came to be with us. To comfort us and let us know we weren't alone.

I think that's what it was like for Jesus to leave the crowd and go with Jairus. He was going to heal the girl. But that was only part of it. And when I saw the painting that day, I was remembering the kind of incarnate God who has all the time in the world.

Over the years, I'd lost the forest for the trees—so focused on small things that I didn't see the big picture anymore. I'd gotten too confident I was right about God. And I'd started believing being correct about faith was the most important thing. I wanted to help people be happy and safe and whole, and to some extent that happened. But I also ended up burdening them with lists, rules, and external authorities.

Then I got overwhelmed by suffering, and some of the church that claimed to embody Jesus hurt my family and others. The Jesus I was hearing about then always seemed mad or disappointed. And in real life and on social media, Jesus' followers were starting to seem like real jerks. I was discouraged at the battles I saw Christians fighting and what was getting overlooked. (I still am.)

When I saw that painting, I started recalling a Savior who would risk frustrating his friends and people who had come to see him because love and mercy were more important. A Savior who cared about a grieving father's only daughter and whose heart broke for a mom who had lost a child. It had seemed like the end, but it wasn't.

Back when Moses got to see God on the mountain, God described himself as overflowing with love and kindness and patience and forgiveness (Exodus 34:6-7). He said he judges because he values justice and cares about the oppressed going free. The Divine notices when the powerful are greedy and the poor go without. Yet the headline is love beyond imagining. It's mercy, not for one or two generations, but for a thousand.

If the rest of the stories about him are any indication, Jesus could have healed the little girl without ever leaving the crowd. All he needed was to say the word or think the thought or whatever it is a deity does to make things happen. But he went to them. And brought life where death had been. Beauty for ashes. I was starting to remember. It was like coming home.

A week later, I went back to buy the painting. It hangs in my dining room, an Ebenezer of a time when hope got rekindled. William Joseph Seymour once wrote, "The Pentecostal power, when you sum it all up, is just more of God's love. If it does not bring more of God's love it is simply a counterfeit."[6]

Admitting We Don't Understand

Which brings us back to Job. He kept maintaining his love for God, his innocence, and his sense of welcome to beg for answers and relief. And that's when God showed up. He addressed Job directly, as if young Elihu hadn't said a word. God was honoring Job's appeal for a chance to ask his questions in person. God takes our complaints and sorrow seriously. And while it's unlikely we'll hear the audible voice of the Divine, the Spirit is near to those who weep and wait for deliverance.

God didn't explain why injustice is sometimes unchecked or the poor and righteous sometimes suffer. He didn't disclose his debate with the Accuser. He talked about his power, the beauty of creation, and how far beyond any human's ability to create, control, or fathom it all is. He said the wicked would be shaken out but didn't mention when that would be.

Then he asked if Job knew how to make a glacier, lead constellations, control the weather, or provide for animals. His questions weren't rhetorical. God demanded an answer. And Job was quick to confess his smallness before God.

God wasn't finished. He started talking about a creature called Behemoth, who was so powerfully built he didn't need to fear rapids, and Leviathan, who had a hide like metal and razor-sharp teeth. After addressing the created world and the problem of evil, God was surfacing the idea of mortality and death with dramatic descriptions of creatures Job would have heard of even if he'd never seen them. Galbraith Hall Todd says, "In the mythological imagery of Egypt and the ancient East, the hippopotamus [behemoth] and the crocodile [leviathan] always represented death and the realms of the dead."[7]

Job acknowledged he'd been talking about things he didn't (and couldn't) fully understand. And he returned to where he began, with dust and ashes marking his suffering and also his humility before God. And that's when things get interesting. Because so far, it seemed God had sided with Job's friends. But he hadn't.

After some stern language with Job, God turned toward his three friends, again ignoring young Elihu. He said they should beg Job to pray for them. They'd been misrepresenting God, and he was mad about it. Job needed to acknowledge his creatureliness and the extent to which God's ways were beyond him; but he was right about the realities of injustice and his friends had been spouting a lot of nonsense in God's name.

The Mosaic law was full of promises of God's blessing for righteousness and punishment for evil. It promised righteousness would be rewarded and evil punished. Their error was to stubbornly maintain priestly tradition that proclaimed punishment for evil and injustice when the moment required a prophetic posture that was better suited to brokenness and suffering. They refused to move out of that orientation even when circumstances demanded it.

They were afraid to entertain the reality of disorientation that was right in front of them. It kept them from admitting they didn't understand. Holy reorientation was impossible until they did. Modern-day comforters teaching harmful things about God and people often claim to be speaking for God as Job's friends did. The situation wasn't hopeless for Job's friends, and it isn't for us. When they confessed that sometimes bad things happen and they didn't know why, they were set free.

Warren Wiersbe says the secret to Job's wisdom was his willingness to stay with his questions even in the face of suffering and God's apparent absence. He "trusted God in spite of Satan, circumstances, friends, or loved ones. His faith at times wavered, and sometimes he accused God, but he still endured."[8] James's epistle celebrates Job as model of patience and a revelation of God's mercy (James 5:11). Suffering invites us to stop and notice where we are, to pay attention to the landscape, and to watch for glimpses of the Spirit.

Job's drama concludes with God showering Job with wealth, restoring his community, and more children. These are the same number as before, seven sons and three daughters. I wish the biblical author would have given us some insight into what became of Job's wife, who lost as much as he did. But it is lovely we are given the names of his daughters, who received an inheritance along with their brothers, which was unusual in the ancient world (Job 42:14-15). Job lived to meet his great grandchildren. While none of that goodness lessens his suffering, his restoration and consolation matter. And it was only possible on the other side of hard questions that defied easy answers.

My daughter discovered she was pregnant a few months after her miscarriage. And at their first doctor's visit, she and Craig learned she was carrying twins. They were shocked, elated, and a little overwhelmed. When she posted they were expecting a boy and a girl, she included Isaiah's words about a loving God showering double blessings after loss and shame. "Instead of your shame you will have a double portion, And instead of humiliation they will shout for joy over their portion. Therefore they will possess a double portion in their land, Everlasting joy will be theirs" (Isaiah 61:7 NASB). New lives don't make losing their first child any less significant, and it is also true that loss can't possibly diminish the reality that the lives of Sutton and William are extravagant gifts. Their lives *all* matter. Great grief and overwhelming joy can coexist. Death and loss don't get the final say.

Making Things New

Over the past months, I've been making a prayer cloth. I started with a finger labyrinth. Taking cues from *kintsugi*, the Japanese art of repairing broken pottery with gold, I stitched the labyrinth's path in gold thread. Later, on the empty parts of the cloth around the labyrinth, I pieced together strips of fabric I'd torn when grieving. I'd torn some after the loss of my grandson. I'd torn others after bad news, disappointments, disconnection, mass shootings, and while interceding for others. I wanted all those threads to get woven together into something new.

I stitched while talking with God, while streaming Sunday morning worship, while watching reruns. I stitched in the middle of the night when worries kept me awake, while crying, while hoping, while praying for my grandchildren. My needle traced the tattered edges and slowly shaped them into wholeness; it wove colors into new patterns, interlacing shimmers of gold into frayed fabric. And it has taken time. I could have finished the project in an hour using a sewing machine. But the time is the point.

Every stitch is a prayer for healing and renewal. Every knot is a decision to tend wounds and a witness of the tender work of repair. The prayers are rooted deep in me, and I'm convinced they're embedded in the fabric, too. Every thread is a testament announcing broken things can sometimes be mended. That redemption is possible. That new life can follow loss. That hope and joy can be reborn.

Collage Practice

First engage in the tearing practice from the end of chapter two, or use some strips of paper you tore in that exercise. Give yourself all the time you need to honor the sorrow or loss you experienced and the freedom to express it.

When you feel ready, consider what changes or memories you will carry forward. Let yourself dream of what you hope will unfold on the other side of loss. You could even try turning your attention toward the good gifts within or beyond your grief.

You'll want to have some glue or tape, markers, colored pencils, or crayons available. Using some of the bits of torn paper from the tearing exercise and any of your other supplies, create a collage on art paper or in a journal of what you hope for and what you're grateful for. Notice the torn paper—which expressed your loss—gets to become something new.

I encourage you to welcome your inner eight-year-old. Try not to edit your work as you go or have a predetermined goal you're overly attached to. Let your creating be a form of welcoming all that is, grief alongside gratitude.

When you finish your collage, notice what hopes and dreams emerged. What changes or restoration do you want to pursue? What is yours to do to cultivate more goodness?

What surprised you about this exercise? Where did you sense goodness or comfort? Do you want to say anything to God about it?

Collage Practice for Children and Families

Engage in the tearing activity from chapter two, or use some torn strips that you've saved.

Have art, construction, or printer paper available on which to create a collage. Have some glue or tape, markers, colored pencils or crayons, photographs of loved ones, and magazines to cut words or pictures out of available.

Invite the child or children to remember the thing they are grieving or the ones they've lost, alongside any good and happy things about this time. Have they noticed any silver linings or bright spots in what's been hard? It's okay if they have and it's also okay if they haven't.

Also invite them to dream about what their world can be like in the future. With all that in mind, invite them to create a collage to illustrate the hopes and dreams of the future using the torn strips. The sad and broken pieces can become part of creating something new. Let them know that they can invite God into what they are making if they want to. They can ask God to heal or for any help they need.

What do they want to be sure to remember about the person or thing that is lost? Wonder with them about how they can play a role in making the world better, more beautiful, and kinder.

Acknowledgments

THANKS TO ALL who read early drafts of what became *Hopeful Lament.* I am especially grateful to Becky Grisell, Kaisa Stenberg-Lee, Kristin Hamilton, Jenn Bibb, Alicia Munro, Lacy Finn Borgo, Jackie Roese, Gena St. David, Ellie Beatty, and Daniel Ting for your generous and invaluable insights. Thank you for cheering me on!

To Meghan Smith for her love and friendship for my family over many years and for her wonderful work taking my author photographs. I'm thankful you're part of our story.

To Cindy Bunch and the team at IVP who believed in this project and helped make it better. I couldn't have done this without you.

To Anne Province who hosted countless safe, spiritual conversations that have formed and freed me. Thank you for helping me see God's kindness and love with fresh eyes.

To Jenny Rose Ford who has cried with me, laughed with me, and delivered iced coffees when they were most needed. You have been a faithful friend as I've found hope again, rebuilding brick by brick. I'm glad you're in the world, friend.

To Kyle, Torey, and Craig, you have survived these things with me. Thank you all for your love and support during this work. I'm profoundly grateful you've allowed me to share some of our stories here. I hope you'll feel loved and honored by how I've told them.

Notes

Introduction: When the Last Resort Is the Only Choice

[1]Matt Miller, "*WandaVision* Episode Eight's Quote About Grief Has Become the Show's Defining Moment," *Esquire*, March 3, 2021, www.esquire.com/entertainment/tv/a35713623/wandavision-episode-8-grief-quote-explained/.

[2]Alisha Grauso, "WandaVision's Perfect Line About Grief Fixes the MCU's Problem with Death," Screen Rant, March 1, 2021, https://screenrant.com/wandavision-grief-line-mcu-death-problem-fix/.

[3]World Health Organization, "Rolling Updates on Coronavirus Disease (Covid-19)," WHO, July 30, 2020, www.who.int/emergencies/diseases/novel-coronavirus-2019/events-as-they-happen.

[4]Domenico Cucinotta and Maurizio Vanelli, "WHO Declares COVID-19 a Pandemic," *Acta Biomedica* 91, no. 1 (March 2020), https://pubmed.ncbi.nlm.nih.gov/32191675/.

[5]Peter D. Kramer, "Burials Without Funerals, Grief Without Hugs: Coronavirus Is Changing How We Say Goodbye," *USA Today*, April 2, 2020, www.usatoday.com/story/news/nation/2020/04/02/funerals-during-coronavirus-pandemic-no-hugs-big-gatherings/5102855002/.

[6]Center for Systems Science and Engineering (CSSE), Covid-19 Dashboard, Johns Hopkins University, accessed November 5, 2022, https://coronavirus.jhu.edu/map.html.

[7]Stephanie Soucheray, "Amid Covid-19, US Life Expectancy Sees Biggest Drop Since WWII," Center for Infectious Disease Research and Policy, February 18, 2021, www.cidrap.umn.edu/news-perspective/2021/02/amid-covid-19-us-life-expectancy-sees-biggest-drop-wwii.

[8]Olivia B. Waxman and Chris Wilson, "How the Coronavirus Death Toll Compares to Other Deadly Events From American History," *Time*, September 1, 2021, https://time.com/5815367/coronavirus-deaths-comparison/.

[9]"Covid Update: Hotline Continues to Hear from Children, Those Concerned for Their Safety," Rape, Abuse & Incest National Network (Rainn), June 19, 2020, www.rainn.org/news/covid-update-hotline-continues-hear-children-those-concerned-their-safety.

[10]Juliana Menasce Horowitz et al., "Amid National Reckoning, Americans Divided on Whether Increased Focus on Race Will Lead to Major Policy Change," Pew Research Center, October 6, 2020, www.pewresearch.org/social-trends/2020/10/06/amid-national-reckoning-americans-divided-on-whether-increased-focus-on-race-will-lead-to-major-policy-change/.

[11]Samuel Corum, "'Unite the Right' Rally in Charlottesville Turns Violent," ABC News, August 12, 2017, https://abcnews.go.com/US/photos/white-nationalists-counterprotesters-clash-charlottesville-49178539/image-56939951.

[12]Larry Buchanan, Quoctrung Bui, and Jugal K. Patel, "Black Lives Matter May Be the Largest Movement in U.S. History," *New York Times*, July 3, 2020, www.nytimes.com/interactive/2020/07/03/us/george-floyd-protests-crowd-size.html.

[13]Kimmy Yam, "Anti-Asian Hate Crimes Increased by Nearly 150% in 2020, Mostly in N.Y. and L.A., New Report Says," NBC News, March 9, 2021, www.nbcnews.com/news/asian-america/anti-asian-hate-crimes-increased-nearly-150-2020-mostly-n-n1260264.

[14]Keith McMillan et al., "Biden, Harris Denounce Attacks on Asian Americans," *Washington Post*, March 19, 2021, www.washingtonpost.com/nation/2021/03/19/atlanta-shooting-updates/.

[15]"Why Has the Syrian War Lasted 11 Years?," BBC, March 15, 2022, www.bbc.com/news/world-middle-east-35806229.

[16]Hannah Beech, Saw Nang, and Marlise Simons, "'Kill All You See': In a First, Myanmar Soldiers Tell of Rohingya Slaughter," *New York Times*, October 19, 2021, www.nytimes.com/2020/09/08/world/asia/myanmar-rohingya-genocide.html.

[17]Hadas Gold et al., "Hamas Predicts Mideast Ceasefire Is 'Imminent' Amid Growing Global Pressure," *CNN*, May 19, 2021, www.cnn.com/2021/05/19/middleeast/israel-palestinian-conflict-wednesday-intl/index.html.

[18]"Lament" in English from 1500–2019, Google Books Ngram Viewer, accessed October 1, 2022, https://books.google.com/ngrams/graph?content=lament&year_start=1500&year_end=2019&corpus=en-2012&smoothing=4&case_insensitive=true.

[19]Charles Taylor, *A Secular Age* (Cambridge, MA: Harvard University Press, 2007), 42.

[20]Neil Howe, "Millennials and the Loneliness Epidemic," *Forbes*, May 3, 2019, www.forbes.com/sites/neilhowe/2019/05/03/millennials-and-the-loneliness-epidemic/?sh=119df7e47676.

[21]Henri Nouwen, *Spiritual Direction: Wisdom for the Long Walk of Faith* (New York: HarperOne, 2006), 10-11.

[22]John O'Donohue, *To Bless the Space Between Us: A Book of Blessings* (New York: Doubleday, 2008), 15.

[23]Jan Richardson, *Circle of Grace: A Book of Blessings for the Seasons* (Orlando, FL: Wanton Gospeller Press, 2015), 102-3.

1. Ashes for Beauty

[1]*What Dreams May Come*, directed by Vincent Ward (Interscope Communications, 1998), accessed June 3, 2022, www.imdb.com/title/tt0120889/characters/nm0000245.

[2]James K. A. Smith, *You Are What You Love: The Spiritual Power of Habit* (Grand Rapids, MI: Brazos Press, 2016), 133.

[3]Bessel van der Kolk, *The Body Keeps the Score: Brain, Mind, and Body in the Healing of Trauma* (New York: Viking, 2014), 2-3.

[4]Claire Bidwell Smith, *Anxiety, the Missing Stage of Grief: A Revolutionary Approach to Understanding and Healing the Impact of Loss* (New York: De Capo Press, 2018), 167.

[5]Van der Kolk, *The Body Keeps the Score*, 3.

[6]Thomas Lewis, Fari Amini, and Richard Lannon, *A General Theory of Love* (New York: Random House, 2000), 45-46.

[7]Resmaa Menakem, *My Grandmother's Hands: Racialized Trauma and the Pathway to Mending Our Hearts and Bodies* (Las Vegas, NV: Central Recovery Press, 2017), 19-20.

[8]The card's designer, Emily McDowell, has built her company on creating greeting cards that major in empathy instead of trite sentiment.

[9]Barbara Brown Taylor, *Learning to Walk in the Dark* (New York: HarperOne, 2014), 8.

[10]N. T. Wright, *God and the Pandemic: A Christian Reflection on the Coronavirus and Its Aftermath* (Grand Rapids, MI: Zondervan Reflective, 2020), 20, emphasis in original.

[11]Eugene H. Peterson, *A Long Obedience in the Same Direction: Discipleship in an Instant Society* (Downers Grove, IL: InterVarsity Press, 2000), 137.

2. How Grieving Got Lost

[1]C. S. Lewis, *A Grief Observed* (New York: Harper Collins, 1996), introduction.

[2]Cori Doerrfeld, *The Rabbit Listened* (New York: Dial Books for Young Readers, 2018).

[3]Sue Monk Kidd, *Dance of the Dissident Daughter: A Woman's Journey from Christian Tradition to the Sacred Feminine* (New York: HarperOne, 2016), 39.

[4]N. T. Wright, *God and the Pandemic: A Christian Reflection on the Coronavirus and its Aftermath* (Zondervan Reflective, Grand Rapids, 2020), 26.

[5]Diane Langberg, *Suffering and the Heart of God: How Trauma Destroys and Christ Restores* (Greensboro, NC: New Growth Press, 2015), 75.

[6]Sue Monk Kidd, *When the Heart Waits: Spiritual Direction for Life's Sacred Questions* (San Francisco: Harper & Row, 1990), 27.

[7]Tobin Hart, *The Secret Spiritual World of Children* (Maui, HI: Inner Ocean, 2003), 211.

[8]Katherine May, *Wintering: The Power of Rest and Retreat in Difficult Times* (New York: Riverhead Books, 2020), 13.

[9]Dylan Scott, "The Pandemic Changed the Trajectory of America's Overdose and Suicide Crises," Vox, August 12, 2021, www.vox.com/policy-and-politics/2021/8/12/22619913/covid-19-us-suicides-drug-overdoses-2020-fentanyl.

[10]Langberg, *Suffering and the Heart of God*, 149.

[11]Soong-Chan Rah, *Prophetic Lament: A Call for Justice in Troubled Times* (Downers Grove, IL: InterVarsity Press, 2015), 67.

[12]Henri Nouwen, *Spiritual Direction: Wisdom for the Long Walk of Faith* (New York: HarperOne, 2006), 7-8.

[13]Kelsey Crowe and Emily McDowell, *There Is No Good Card for This: What to Say and Do When Life Is Scary, Awful, and Unfair to People You Love* (New York: HarperOne, 2017), 155-58.

[14]Merissa Nathan Gerson, *Forget Prayers, Bring Cake: A Single Woman's Guide to Grieving* (San Rafael, CA: Mandala, 2021), 32.

[15]Perry Como, "Accentuate the Positive," Track 2 on *Saturday Night with Mr. C*, RCA Records, 1958, Spotify, https://open.spotify.com/track/5WMt98xu4lnKVp5PgeuecD?si=b957da4f8deb402f.

[16]Anthony Giddens, *Consequences of Modernity* (Stanford, CA: Stanford University Press, 1990), 4.

[17]Abram Van Engen, "How America Became 'A City Upon a Hill,'" *Humanities* 41, no. 1 (Winter 2020): www.neh.gov/article/how-america-became-city-upon-hill.

[18]Ron Elving, "Norman Vincent Peale Was a Conservative Hero Known Well Beyond His Era," NPR, July 24, 2020, www.npr.org/2020/07/24/894967922/norman-vincent-peale-was-a-conservative-hero-known-well-beyond-his-era.

[19]Clarke A. Chambers, "The Belief in Progress in Twentieth-Century America," *Journal of the History of Ideas* 19, no. 2 (1958): 197, www.jstor.org/stable/2707935.

[20]Francis Fukuyama, *The End of History and the Last Man* (New York: Free Press, 1992).

[21]Nancy C. Lee, *Lyrics of Lament: From Tragedy to Transformation* (Minneapolis: Fortress Press, 2010), 153.

[22]John. R. Lampe, "Bosnian War: European History [1992-1995]," *Britannica*, accessed December 18, 2021, www.britannica.com/event/Bosnian-War.

[23]History.com Editors, "Columbine Shooting," History website, May 25, 2022, www.history.com/topics/1990s/columbine-high-school-shootings.

[24]Antonio Planas, "2 People Killed in World Trade Center on 9/11 Identified with DNA Ahead of 20th Anniversary," NBC News, September 8, 2021, www.nbcnews.com/news/us-news/2-people-killed-world-trade-center-9-11-identified-dna-n1278723.

[25]Renae Merle, "A Guide to the Financial Crisis—10 Years Later," *Washington Post*, September 10, 2018, www.washingtonpost.com/business/economy/a-guide-to-the-financial-crisis--10-years-later/2018/09/10/114b76ba-af10-11e8-a20b-5f4f84429666_story.html.

[26]Pew Research Report, "America's Shrinking Middle Class: A Close Look at Changes Within Metropolitan Areas," Pew Research Center, May 11, 2016, www.pewresearch.org/social-trends/2016/05/11/americas-shrinking-middle-class-a-close-look-at-changes-within-metropolitan-areas/.

[27]Sam Roberts, "Facing a Financial Pinch, and Moving In With Mom and Dad," *The New York Times*, March 21, 2010, www.nytimes.com/2010/03/22/nyregion/22singles.html.

[28]Elving, "Norman Vincent Peale Was a Conservative Hero."

[29]Gwenda Blair, "How Norman Vincent Peale Taught Donald Trump to Worship Himself: The Magnate's Biographer Explains the Spiritual Guide Behind His Relentless Self-Confidence," *Politico*, October 06, 2015, www.politico.com/magazine/story/2015/10/donald-trump-2016-norman-vincent-peale-213220/.

[30]Blair, "How Norman Vincent Peale Taught Donald Trump."

[31]Karen Hao, "The Facebook Whistleblower Says Its Algorithms Are Dangerous. Here's Why," *MIT Technology Review*, October 5, 2021, www.technologyreview.com/2021/10/05/1036519/facebook-whistleblower-frances-haugen-algorithms/.

[32]Hao, "The Facebook Whistleblower"

[33]Zygmunt Bauman, *Modernity and the Holocaust* (Ithaca, NY: Cornell University Press, 2000), 13-15.

[34]Zygmunt Bauman, "Zygmunt Bauman: Social Media Are a Trap," interview by Ricardo de Querol, *El País*, January 25, 2016, https://english.elpais.com/elpais/2016/01/19/inenglish/1453208692_424660.html.

[35]Merold Westphal, *Whose Community? Which Interpretation?: Philosophical Hermeneutics for the Church* (Grand Rapids, MI: Baker Academic, 2009), 129.

[36]Rah, *Prophetic Lament,* 67.

[37]Richard G. Tedeschi and Lawrence G. Calhoun, "Posttraumatic Growth: Conceptual Foundations and Empirical Evidence," *Psychological Inquiry* 15, no. 1 (2004): 4.

[38]C. S. Lewis, *A Grief Observed* (New York: Harper Collins 1996), 1.

[39]William Nicholson, screenplay author, *Shadowlands*, directed by Richard Attenborough (1993; Price Entertainment), www.imdb.com/title/tt0108101/.

3. Learning to Speak Sadness

[1]Tom Lanham, "'We Can't Run Away Anymore': Hurray for the Riff Raff Embraces *Life on Earth*," February 18, 2022, *Paste*, www.pastemagazine.com/music/hurray-for-the-riff-raff-interview-life-on-earth/?utm_source=PMNTNL&utm_medium=email&utm_campaign=220219.

[2]Walter Brueggemann, *Spirituality of the Psalms* (Minneapolis: Fortress Press, 2002), 13.

[3]Mark Vroegop, *Dark Clouds, Deep Mercy: Discovering the Grace of Lament* (Wheaton, IL: Crossway 2019), 21.

[4]Michael Card, *The Hidden Face of God: Finding the Missing Door to the Father Through Lament* (Colorado Springs, CO: NavPress, 2007), 26.

[5]Heather Hawk Feinberg, *Crying Is Like the Rain: A Story of Mindfulness and Feelings* (Thomaston, ME: Tilbury House, 2020), 31.

[6]Liila Taruffi and Stefan, "The Paradox of Music-Evoked Sadness: An Online Survey," *PLoS ONE* 9(10): e110490, doi:10.1371/journal.pone.0110490.

[7]J. K. Rowling, *Harry Potter and the Half-Blood Prince* (New York: Levine, 2005), 512.

[8]J. R. R. Tolkien, *The Fellowship of the Ring* (Boston: Houghton Mifflin, 1956), 374.

[9]Wilhelm Gesenius and Samuel Prideaux Tregelles, *Gesenius' Hebrew and Chaldee Lexicon to the Old Testament Scriptures* (Bellingham, WA: Logos Bible Software, 2003).

[10]James H. Cone, *The Cross and the Lynching Tree* (Maryknoll, NY: Orbis Books, 2011), xiii.

[11]Cone, *The Cross and the Lynching Tree*, 134.

[12]Cone, *The Cross and the Lynching Tree*, 12.

[13]James Weldon Johnson, *God's Trombones: Seven Negro Sermons in Verse* (New York: Penguin Books, 2008), xxiii.

[14]Anne K. Capel, "Relief of Mourners and Funerary Repast," in *Mistress of the House, Mistress of Heaven: Women in Ancient Egypt*, ed. Anne K. Capel and Glenn E. Markoe (New York: Hudson Hills Press, 1996), 93-94.

[15]M. G. Easton, *Illustrated Bible Dictionary and Treasury of Biblical History, Biography, Geography, Doctrine, and Literature* (New York: Harper & Brothers, 1893), 480.

[16]Capel "Relief of Mourners and Funerary Repast," 94.

[17]Capel "Relief of Mourners and Funerary Repast," 94.

[18]J. Tyldesley, *Daughters of Isis: Women of Ancient Egypt* (London: Viking, 1994), 132, quoted in Anne K. Capel, "Relief of Mourners and Funerary Repast," in *Mistress of the House, Mistress of Heaven: Women in Ancient Egypt*, ed. Anne K. Capel and Glenn E. Markoe (New York: Hudson Hills Press, 1996), 94.

[19]Sarah Hucal, "Professional Mourners Still Exist in Greece," *Deutsche Welle* (dw.com), November 15, 2020, www.dw.com/en/professional-mourners-keep-an-ancient-tradition-alive-in-greece/a-55572864.

[20]Louisa Lim, "Belly Dancing for the Dead: A Day With China's Top Mourner," *NPR*, June, 26, 2013, www.npr.org/2013/06/26/195565696/belly-dancing-for-the-dead-a-day-with-chinas-top-mourner.

[21]Lim, "Belly Dancing for the Dead."

[22]"Professional Mourners Who Are Hired to 'Mourn' at Funerals," Citizen TV Kenya, November 23, 2018, www.youtube.com/watch?v=GlH8pyeOz9I.

[23]Zakes Mda, *Ways of Dying* (New York: Picador, 1995), chap. 1.

[24]*Funeral in Berlin*, directed by Guy Hamilton, (United Kingdom: Paramount Pictures, 1966).

[25]Hank Williams, "Nobody's Lonesome For Me (Acetate Version 1)," on *Pictures From Life's Other Side: The Man and His Music In Rare Recordings and Photos* (2019—Remaster), Spotify.

[26]Anonymous and Evan V. Symon, "I'm Paid To Mourn At Funerals (And It's A Growing Industry)," *Cracked*, March 21, 2016, www.cracked.com/personal-experiences-1994-i-am-professional-mourner-6-realities-my-job.html.

4. Letting Sorrow Be a Conversation with God

[1]Walter Brueggemann, *Spirituality of the Psalms* (Minneapolis: Fortress Press, 2002), 68.

[2]Brueggemann, *Spirituality of the Psalms*, 47.

[3]Nancy C. Lee, *Lyrics of Lament: From Tragedy to Transformation* (Minneapolis: Fortress Press, 2010), 73-74.

[4]Richard J. Foster, *Streams of Living Water: Essential Practices from the Six Great Traditions of Christian Faith* (New York: HarperCollins, 1998), 118, emphasis in original.

[5]Foster, *Streams of Living Water*, 118.

[6]Foster, *Streams of Living Water*, 119.

[7]Osheta Moore, *Dear White Peacemakers: Dismantling Racism with Grit and Grace* (Harrisonburg, VA: Herald Press, 2021), 74.

[8]Abraham Lincoln, "Proclamation 97—Appointing a Day of National Humiliation, Fasting, and Prayer," The American Presidency Project, March 30, 1863, www.presidency.ucsb.edu/documents/proclamation-97-appointing-day-national-humiliation-fasting-and-prayer.

[9]Margaret Guenther, *Holy Listening: The Art of Spiritual Direction* (Cambridge, MA: Cowley Publications, 1992), 130.

[10]Thomas Merton, *Spiritual Direction and Meditation* (Collegeville, MN: Liturgical Press, 1987), 35.

[11]Johannes P. Louw and Eugene Albert Nida, *Greek-English Lexicon of the New Testament: Based on Semantic Domains* (New York: United Bible Societies, 1996), 514.

[12]John of the Cross, in *An Anthology of Christian Mysticism*, 2nd ed., edited by Harvey D. Egan (Collegeville, MN: Liturgical Press, 1996), 461.

[13]Lee, *Lyrics of Lament*, 184.

[14]Terry Tempest Williams, *Finding Beauty in a Broken World* (New York: Vintage Books, 2008), 9.

[15]Jan Richardson, *Sparrow: A Book of Life and Death and Life* (Orlando, FL: Wanton Gospeller Press, 2020), xiii.

[16]Gena St. David, *The Brain and the Spirit: Unlocking the Transformative Potential of the Story of Christ* (Eugene, OR: Cascade Books, 2021), 149, emphasis in original.

[17]Aundi Kolber, *Try Softer: A Fresh Approach to Move Us out of Anxiety, Stress, and Survival Mode—and into a Life of Connection and Joy* (Carol Stream, IL: Tyndale Momentum, 2020), 63.

[18]St. David, *The Brain and the Spirit*, 151.

[19]St. David, *The Brain and the Spirit*, 155.

5. Grief Work

[1]Identifying details have been changed to protect the anonymity of this person. That is the case whenever I reference the stories of those I host in spiritual direction.

[2]Aubrey Sampson, *Louder Song: Listening for Hope in the Midst of Lament* (Colorado Springs: NavPress, 2019), 4.

[3]Maya Tamir et al., "The Secret to Happiness: Feeling Good or Feeling Right?" *Journal of Experimental Psychology* 146, no. 10 (2017): 1448.

[4]Tamir et al., "The Secret to Happiness," 1456-57.

[5]Sasha Sagan, "9/11 and Everything After: On Bearing Witness to History Through the Eyes of My Daughter," LitHub, September 10, 2021, https://lithub.com/9-11-and-everything-after-on-bearing-witness-to-history-through-the-eyes-of-my-daughter.

[6]Austin Channing Brown, *I'm Still Here: Black Dignity in a World Made for Whiteness* (New York: Convergent, 2081), 57.

[7]Suleika Jaouad, "No. 3 – On Touching the Truth – Nadia Bolz-Weber," *The Isolation Journals*, October 21, 2020, www.theisolationjournals.com/blog/nadiabolzweber.

[8]N. T. Wright, *God and the Pandemic: A Christian Reflection on the Coronavirus and its Aftermath* (Grand Rapids, MI: Zondervan Reflective, 2020), 31.

[9]Fleming Rutledge, *Advent: The Once and Future Coming of Jesus Christ* (Grand Rapids, MI: Eerdmans, 2018), 108-9.

[10]I was introduced to the idea of metabolizing pain and trauma in Resmaa Menakem's book *My Grandmother's Hands: Racialized Trauma and the Pathway to Mending Our Hearts and Bodies* (Las Vegas, NV: Central Recovery Press, 2017).

[11]"Pantoum," Glossary of Poetic Terms, Poetry Foundation, accessed September 30, 2021, www.poetryfoundation.org/learn/glossary-terms/pantoum.

[12]Edward Hirsch, "Edward Hirsch's A Poet's Glossary," Poets.org, accessed September 30, 2021, https://poets.org/edward-hirschs-poets-glossary.

[13]Johannes P. Louw and Eugene Albert Nida, *Greek-English Lexicon of the New Testament: Based on Semantic Domains* (New York: United Bible Societies, 1996), 25.246.

[14]James Swanson, *Dictionary of Biblical Languages with Semantic Domains: Greek (New Testament)* (Oak Harbor, WA: Logos Research Systems, Inc., 1997).

[15]Louw and Nida, *Greek-English Lexicon of the New Testament*, 349.

[16]Eugene Peterson, *A Long Obedience in the Same Direction: Discipleship in an Instant Society* (Downers Grove, IL: InterVarsity Press, 2000), 144.

6. Trauma and the Courage to Lament

[1]Lisa Miller, *The Spiritual Child: The New Science on Parenting for Health and Lifelong Thriving* (New York: St. Martin's Press, 2015), 40.

[2]Thomas Lewis, Fari Amini, and Richard Lannon, *A General Theory of Love* (New York: Random House, 2000), 27.

[3]Gena St. David, *The Brain and the Spirit: Unlocking the Transformative Potential of the Story of Christ* (Eugene, OR: Cascade Books, 2021), 11.

[4]Lewis, Amini, and Lannon, *A General Theory of Love*, 26.

[5]Aundi Kolber, *Try Softer: A Fresh Approach to Move Us out of Anxiety, Stress, and Survival Mode—And into a Life of Connection and Joy* (Carol Stream, IL: Tyndale Momentum, 2020), 33.

[6]Bessel van der Kolk, *The Body Keeps the Score: Brain, Mind, and Body in the Healing of Trauma* (New York: Viking, 2014), 84.

[7]Van der Kolk, *The Body Keeps the Score*, 84.

[8]Kolber, *Try Softer*, 33.

[9]Resmaa Menakem, *My Grandmother's Hands: Racialized Trauma and the Pathway to Mending Our Hearts and Bodies* (Las Vegas, NV: Central Recovery Press, 2017), xiv.

[10]Van der Kolk, *The Body Keeps the Score*, 30.

[11]Kolber, *Try Softer*, 73.

[12]Van der Kolk, *The Body Keeps the Score*, 21.

[13]Kolber, *Try Softer*, 87-88.

[14]Claire Bidwell Smith, *Anxiety: The Missing Stage of Grief: A Revolutionary Approach to Understanding and Healing the Impact of Loss* (New York: Da Capo Press, 2018), 188.

[15]Van der Kolk, *The Body Keeps the Score*, 275.

[16]Van der Kolk, *The Body Keeps the Score*, 275.

[17]Smith, *Anxiety*, 19.

[18]Smith, *Anxiety*, 79-81.

[19]Lewis, Amini, and Lannon, *A General Theory of Love*, 85.

[20]Van der Kolk, *The Body Keeps the Score*, 13.

[21]Smith, *Anxiety*, 58.

Terra Divina Practice

[1]Allison Aubrey, "Forest Bathing: A Retreat To Nature Can Boost Immunity And Mood," *NPR*, July 17, 2017, www.npr.org/sections/health-shots/2017/07/17/536676954/forest-bathing-a-retreat-to-nature-can-boost-immunity-and-mood.

[2]Cole Arthur Riley, *This Here Flesh: Spirituality, Liberation, and the Stories That Make Us* (New York: Convergent, 2022), 18.

7. Lamenting When Community Is Toxic

[1]*The Rise and Fall of Mars Hill*, produced by Mike Cosper, podcast, www.christianitytoday.com/ct/podcasts/rise-and-fall-of-mars-hill/.

[2]Chuck DeGroat, *When Narcissism Comes to Church: Healing Your Community From Emotional and Spiritual Abuse* (Downers Grove, IL: InterVarsity Press, 2020), 5.

[3]DeGroat, *When Narcissism Comes to Church*, 69, 83.

[4]DeGroat, *When Narcissism Comes to Church*, 14.

[5]Bessel van der Kolk, *The Body Keeps the Score: Brain, Mind, and Body in the Healing of Trauma* (New York: Viking, 2014), 220.

[6]DeGroat, *When Narcissism Comes to Church*, 23.

[7]Van der Kolk, *The Body Keeps the Score*, 211.

[8]Van der Kolk, *The Body Keeps the Score*, 211.

[9]DeGroat, *When Narcissism Comes to Church*, 84.

[10]Gena St. David, *The Brain and the Spirit: Unlocking the Transformative Potential of the Story of Christ* (Eugene, OR: Cascade Books, 2021), 7.

[11]St. David, *The Brain and the Spirit*, 7, emphasis added.

[12]Van der Kolk, *The Body Keeps the Score*, 82.

[13]Claire Bidwell Smith, *Anxiety: The Missing Stage of Grief* (New York: Da Capo Press 2018), 23.

[14]Diane Langberg, *Redeeming Power: Understanding Authority and Abuse in the Church* (Grand Rapids, MI: Brazos Press, 2020), 31.

[15]Smith, *Anxiety*, 57.

[16]Langberg, *Redeeming Power*, 72.

[17]Diane Langberg, *Suffering and the Heart of God* (Greensboro, NC: New Growth Press, 2015), 13.

[18]Diana Butler Bass, *Broken We Kneel: Reflections on Faith and Citizenship* (New York: Church Publishing Incorporated, 2019), 8.

[19]Mae Elise Cannon et al., *Forgive Us: Confessions of a Compromised Faith* (Grand Rapids, MI: Zondervan, 2014), 208.

[20]Alexia Salvatierra and Peter Heltzel, *Faith-Rooted Organizing: Mobilizing the Church in Service to the World* (Downers Grove, IL: InterVarsity Press, 2014), 16.

[21]Salvatierra and Heltzel, *Faith-Rooted Organizing*, 16.

[22]Emmanuel Katongole, *Born From Lament: The Theology and Politics of Hope in Africa* (Grand Rapids, MI: Eerdmans 2017), xv.

Grounding Practice

[1]This practice is inspired by several from Aundi Kolber's *Try Softer* and Resmaa Menakem's *My Grandmother's Hands.*

[2]Aundi Kolber, *Try Softer: A Fresh Approach to Move Us out of Anxiety, Stress, and Survival Mode—And into a Life of Connection and Joy* (Carol Stream, IL: Tyndale Momentum, 2020), 111.

[3]Resmaa Menakem, *My Grandmother's Hands: Racialized Trauma and the Pathway to Mending Our Hearts and Bodies* (Las Vegas, NV: Central Recovery Press, 2017), 29.

[4]Menakem, *My Grandmother's Hands*, 30.

[5]Lacy Finn Borgo, *Spiritual Conversations with Children: Listening to God Together* (Downers Grove, IL: InterVarsity Press, 2020), 108.

8. Grieving Together

[1]Syliva Boorstein, "What We Nurture," May 5, 2022 (originally aired May 5, 2011), in *On Being with Krista Tippett*, produced by Krista Tippett, podcast, https://onbeing.org/programs/sylvia-boorstein-what-we-nurture-2022/.

[2]Ernst Jenni and Claus Westermann, *Theological Lexicon of the Old Testament* (Peabody, MA: Hendrickson Publishers, 1997), 1202.

[3]J. Barton Payne, "*2131 רִיחַ*," in *Theological Wordbook of the Old Testament*, ed. R. Laird Harris, Gleason L. Archer Jr., and Bruce K. Waltke (Chicago: Moody Press, 1999), 836.

[4]Julian of Norwich, *Showings*, trans. Edmund Colledge and James Walsh (Mahway, New Jersey: Paulist Press, 1978), 293.

[5]Richard Rohr, "John of the Cross, Part II: The Dark Night," *Center for Action and Contemplation*, July 30, 2015, https://cac.org/daily-meditations/john-cross-part-ii-dark-night-2015-07-30/.

[6]Emily R. Siegel and Cameron Oakes, "The Zoom Shiva: Jewish Funerals and Mourning in the Age of Covid," *NBC*, April 26, 2020, www.nbcnews.com/health/health-care/zoom-shiva-jewish-funerals-mourning-age-covid-n1191806.

[7]Thomas R. Kelly, *A Testament of Devotion* (New York: HarperOne, 1992), 82.

[8]Kelly, *A Testament of Devotion*, 83.

[9]Diane Glancy, *Island of the Innocent: A Consideration of the Book of Job* (Brooklyn: Turtle Point Press, 2020), 47.

[10]Walter Brueggemann, *Spirituality of the Psalms* (Minneapolis, MN: Fortress Press, 2002), 26.

[11]Quoted in Kathleen D. Billman and Daniel L. Migliore, *Rachel's Cry: Prayer of Lament and Rebirth of Hope*, (Eugene, OR: Wipf & Stock, 2006), 8-9.

[12]Adriel Booker, *Grace Like Scarlett: Grieving with Hope After Miscarriage and Loss* (Grand Rapids, MI: Baker Books, 2018), 28.

[13]Booker, *Grace Like Scarlett*, 85.

[14]Sarah Philpott, *Loved Baby: 31 Devotions Helping You Grieve and Cherish Your Child After Pregnancy Loss* (Savage, MN: Broad Street Publishing, 2017), 68.

[15]Philpott, *Loved Baby*, 69-70.

[16]Philpott, *Loved Baby*, 109-110.

[17]"Helping Children Grieve with Khris Ford and Paula D'Arcy," *Paraclete Press Video*, accessed October 7, 2021, https://paracletepressvideostreaming.vhx.tv/products/helping-children-grieve.

Mandala Practice

[1]Christine Valters Paintner and Betsey Beckman, *Awakening the Creative Spirit: Bringing the Arts to Spiritual Direction* (New York: Morehouse Publishing, 2010), 84.

[2]Hildegard of Bingen, *Scivias*, trans. Mother Columba Hart and Jane Bishop (New York: Paulist Press, 1990), 93.

[3]Paintner and Beckman, *Awakening the Creative Spirit*, 84.

9. Children and Loss

[1]Holly Catterton Allen, *Forming Resilient Children: The Role of Spiritual Formation for Healthy Development* (Downers Grove, IL: IVP Academic, 2021), 152.

[2]Allen, *Forming Resilient Children*, 142.

[3]Centers for Disease Control and Prevention, "Marriage and Divorce" data for 2019, CDC, accessed November 8, 2021, www.cdc.gov/nchs/fastats/marriage-divorce.htm.

[4]Allen, *Forming Resilient Children*, 143.

[5]Allen, *Forming Resilient Children*, 143.

[6]David A. Walters, "Grief and Loss: Towards an Existential Phenomenology of Child Spirituality," *International Journal of Children's Spirituality* 13, no. 3 (May 2008): 279.

[7]Walters, "Grief and Loss," 279.

[8]Tobin Hart, *The Secret Spiritual World of Children*, (Maui, HI: Inner Ocean, 2003), 244.

[9]Shelly Melia, "The Role of Faith or Spirituality in a Child's Response to Grief and Loss," in *Bridging Theory and Practice in Children's Spirituality: New Directions for Education, Ministry, and Discipleship*, ed. Mimi Larson and Robert J. Keeley (Grand Rapids, MI: Zondervan, 2020), 120.

[10]Paraclete Press, "Helping Children Grieve with Khris Ford and Paula D'Arcy," *Paraclete Press Video*, accessed October 7, 2021, https://paracletepressvideostreaming.vhx.tv/products/helping-children-grieve.

[11]Paraclete Press, "Helping Children Grieve."

[12]Paraclete Press, "Helping Children Grieve."

[13]Allen, *Forming Resilient Children*, 43.

[14]Melia, "The Role of Faith or Spirituality," 120, emphasis in original.

[15]Lacy Finn Borgo, *Spiritual Conversations with Children: Listening to God Together* (Downers Grove, IL: InterVarsity Press, 2020), 132.

[16]Walters, "Grief and Loss," 278.

[17]Hart, *The Secret Spiritual World of Children*, 212-13.

[18]Olivia Waxman, "Baby Jessica's Rescue from a Well Capped Off a Terrifying Week in U.S. History," *Time*, October 16, 2017, https://time.com/4980689/baby-jessica-30th-anniversary/.

[19]Melia, "The Role of Faith or Spirituality," 125.

[20]Melia, "The Role of Faith or Spirituality," 125.

[21]Melia, "The Role of Faith or Spirituality," 125-26.

[22]Diane Langberg, *Suffering and the Heart of God: How Trauma Destroys and Christ Restores* (Greensboro, NC: New Growth Press, 2015), 177.

[23]Bianca Quilantan and David Cohen, "Trump Tells Dem Congresswomen: Go Back Where You Came From," *Politico*, July 14, 2019, www.politico.com/story/2019/07/14/Trump-congress-go-back-where-they-came-from-1415692.

[24]Eleanor Goldberg et al., "The Right Way to Talk to Your Kids About School Shootings," theSkimm, May 25, 2022, www.theskimm.com/well/how-to-talk-to-kids-about-school-shootings-4hhctdbv8HXyI1vvFIvHVF?utm_source=newsletter_sm&utm_medium=email.

[25]"AAP-AACAP-CHA Declaration of a National Emergency in Child and Adolescent Mental Health," *AAP*, October 19, 2021, www.aap.org/en/advocacy/child-and-adolescent-healthy-mental-development/aap-aacap-cha-declaration-of-a-national-emergency-in-child-and-adolescent-mental-health/.

[26]American Academy of Child and Adult Psychiatry, "Suicide in Children and Teens," AACAP, June 2021, www.aacap.org/AACAP/Families_and_Youth/Facts_for_Families/FFF-Guide/Teen-Suicide-010.aspx.

[27]Asha Z. Ivey-Stephenson et al., "Suicidal Ideation and Behaviors Among High School Students—Youth Risk Behavior Survey, United States, 2019," CDC, August 21, 2020, www.cdc.gov/mmwr/volumes/69/su/su6901a6.htm?s_cid=su6901a6_w#suggestedcitation.

[28]Ivey-Stephenson et al., "Suicidal Ideation and Behaviors Among High School Students."

[29]Madeleine Roberts, "New CDC Data Shows LGBTQ Youth Are More Likely to be Bullied Than Straight Cisgender Youth," *Human Rights Campaign*, August 26, 2020, www.hrc.org/news/new-cdc-data-shows-lgbtq-youth-are-more-likely-to-be-bullied-than-straight-cisgender-youth.

[30]American Academy of Child and Adult Psychiatry, "Suicide in Children and Teens."

[31]Allen, *Forming Resilient Children*, 160.

[32]Allen, *Forming Resilient Children*, 157-58.

[33]Kate DiCamillo, "For the Eight-Year-Old in You," March 17, 2022, in *On Being with Krista Tippett*, produced by Krista Tippett, podcast, https://onbeing.org/programs/kate-dicamillo-for-the-eight-year-old-in-you/.

[34]DiCamillo, "For the Eight-Year-Old in You."

[35]Eva Eland, *When Sadness Is at Your Door* (New York: Random House, 2019), unnumbered pages.

[36]Paraclete Press, "Helping Children Grieve."

[37]Allen, *Forming Resilient Children*, 111.

[38]Valerie Hess and Marti Watson Garlett, *Habits of a Child's Heart: Raising Your Kids with the Spiritual Disciplines* (Colorado Springs: NavPress, 2004), 19.

[39]Hess and Garlett, *Habits of a Child's Heart*, 27.

[40]Dennis Linn, Sheila Fabricant Linn, and Matthew Linn, *What Is My Song?* (New York: Paulist Press, 2005).

[41]Borgo, *Spiritual Conversations with Children*, 29.

Worry Tree Practice

[1]Khris Ford and Paula D'Arcy use this practice with children who have lost family members. Paraclete Press, "Helping Children Grieve with Khris Ford and Paula D'Arcy," Paraclete Press Video, accessed October 7, 2021, https://paracletepressvideostreaming.vhx.tv/products/helping-children-grieve.

10. Finding the Way Through Lament

[1]Cole Arthur Riley, *This Here Flesh: Spirituality, Liberation, and the Stories That Make Us* (New York: Convergent, 2022), 18.

[2]Howard Thurman, *Jesus and the Disinherited* (Boston: Beacon Press, 1996).

[3]Ibram X. Kendi, *How to Be an Antiracist* (New York: One World, 2019), 23.

[4]Austin Channing Brown, *I'm Still Here: Black Dignity in a World Made for Whiteness* (New York: Convergent, 2081), 101.

[5]Soong-Chan Rah et al., *Forgive Us: Confessions of a Compromised Faith* (Grand Rapids, MI: Zondervan, 2014), 26.

[6]Richard J. Foster, *Streams of Living Water: Essential Practices from the Six Great Traditions of Christian Faith* (New York: HarperOne, 1998), 120.

[7]Galbraith Hall Todd, "Three Questions to a Man in Trouble," *Christianity Today*, November 26, 1956, www.christianitytoday.com/ct/1956/november-26/three-questions-to-man-in-trouble.html.

[8]Warren W. Wiersbe, *Wiersbe's Expository Outlines on the Old Testament* (Wheaton, IL: Victor Books, 1993), Job 42:7-14.

Recommended Reading

Try Softer, Aundi Kolber
Anxiety: The Missing Stage of Grief, Claire Bidwell Smith
This Here Flesh, Cole Arthur Riley
Suffering and the Heart of God, Diane Langberg
A Grief Observed, C. S. Lewis
Brave Lament, Andrew and Christy Bauman
Grace Like Scarlett, Adriel Booker
Lament for a Son, Nicholas Wolterstorff
Prophetic Lament, Soong-Chan Rah
What Is a Girl Worth?, Rachel Denhollander
Learning to Walk in the Dark, Barbara Brown Taylor
The Cure for Sorrow, Jan Richardson
Everything Happens for a Reason and Other Lies I've Loved, Kate Bowler
The Brain and the Spirit, Gena St. David
Spiritual Conversations with Children, Lacy Finn Borgo
I'm Still Here, Austin Channing Brown
The Cross and the Lynching Tree, James H. Cone
My Grandmother's Hands, Resmaa Menakem

Recommended Children's Books

When Sadness Is at Your Door, Eva Eland
The Invisible String, Patrice Karst
Crying Is Like the Rain, Heather Hawk Feinberg
All Will Be Well, Lacy Finn Borgo